Houghton
Mifflin
Harcourt

TEXAS
SCIENCE
FUSion

Assessment Guide

Grade 4

Contents

Unit 3 Matter

Unit 4 Forms of Energy

Unit 5 Electricity and Circuits

Unit 6 Forces and Motion

Unit 11 Plants and Animals

Cumulative Tests

Overview

ScienceFusion provides a variety of instructional tools for meeting the Texas Essential Knowledge and Skills (TEKS) for Science. You may choose to use the interactive Student Edition, the digital curriculum, or a combination of both. The quizzes, tests, and other resources in this Assessment Guide may be used with any of those components.

The *ScienceFusion* assessment options are intended to give you maximum flexibility in assessing what your students know and can do. The program's formative, summative, and performance assessment categories reflect the understanding that assessment is a learning opportunity for students and that all students must demonstrate standards mastery at the end of a school year.

Formative Assessment

At the end of each lesson in the Student Edition, the Brain Check will help you evaluate how well students grasped the concepts taught. The opportunities for students to annotate their Student Edition, including the Active Reading features, can also provide insight into how well students are learning the concepts. At the end of each digital unit, a student self-assessment prompts students to return to areas in which they may need additional work.

The Teacher Edition offers a number of additional tools for formative assessment. Look for the science notebooking strategies Generate Ideas and Summarize Ideas that begin and end many of the two-page sections of the lessons. These strategies provide numerous ways to informally assess whether students are remembering what they read and getting the main ideas. Questions that address a variety of dimensions—including concept development, inquiry skills, and use of reading strategies—are strategically placed throughout each lesson. This Assessment Guide also includes the Observation Checklist, on which you can record observations of students' ability to use science inquiry skills.

Summative Assessment

To help you reinforce and assess mastery of unit objectives, *ScienceFusion* includes both reviews and tests. You will find the Unit Reviews in the Student Edition. This Assessment Guide provides Lesson Quizzes, quizzes for Safety in Science and Science Tools, and Unit Tests. All of these assessment tools include multiple-choice formats that mirror standardized Texas statewide assessment formats. The Unit Tests also contain short-response and extended-response items. Each Assessment Guide unit also provides a two-page TEKS DOK Skill Builder. The Skill Builder includes a TEKS standard, for which are written three test items, one at Depth of Knowledge level 1, one at level 2, and one at level 3, as well as a teacher page that offers guidance in helping students answer the test items. This Assessment Guide also provides two multiple-choice Cumulative Tests that cover all the standards of the program.

Performance Assessment

Performance tasks provide evidence of students' ability to use science inquiry skills and critical thinking to complete an authentic task. A brief performance task is included in the Teacher Edition with each Unit Review. A more comprehensive performance task is provided for each unit in this Assessment Guide as well as for the Safety in Science and Science Tools pages. Each includes teacher directions and a scoring rubric.

Self-Assessment and Portfolio Assessment

Students should be challenged to reflect on their work and monitor their learning. Several checklists are provided for this purpose. Self-Assessment—Active Reading, Experiment/Project Summary Sheet, Self-Assessment—My Science Notebook, Science Experiences Record, and Guide to My Science Portfolio can be used by students to describe or evaluate their own experiences and projects. Opportunities for self-assessment and evaluation are embedded at key points on the digital path.

Online Assessment

All of the quizzes and tests within this Assessment Guide are available in computer-scored format with the *ScienceFusion* online resources. Banks of items from which tests can be built are also available.

Test-Taking Tips

Understandably, students often experience test-related anxiety. Teaching students to apply a number of general test-taking strategies may bolster their confidence and result in improved student performance on formal assessment. As students take a test, they should

- scan the entire test first before answering any questions.

- read the directions slowly and carefully before beginning a section.

- begin with the easiest questions or most familiar material.

- read the question and all answer options before selecting an answer.

- watch out for key words such as *not, least, best, most,* and so on.

- carefully analyze graphs, tables, diagrams, and pictures that accompany items.

- double-check answers to catch and correct errors.

- erase all mistakes completely and write corrections neatly.

Test Preparation

Students perform better on formal assessments when they are well prepared for the testing situation. Here are some things you can do before a test to help your students do their best work.

- Explain the nature of the test to students.

- Suggest that they review the questions at the end of the lessons and the chapter.

- Remind students to get a good night's sleep before the test.

- Discuss why they should eat a balanced meal beforehand.

- Encourage students to relax while they take the test.

Performance Assessment

Teachers today have come to realize that the multiple-choice format of traditional tests, while useful and efficient, cannot provide a complete picture of students' growth in science. Standardized multiple-choice tests cannot fully reveal how students *think and do things*—an essential aspect of science literacy. Performance assessment can provide this missing information and help balance your assessment program. Well-constructed performance assessments provide a window through which teachers may view students' thought processes.

An important feature of performance assessment is that it involves a hands-on activity in which students solve a situational problem. Students often find performance assessment more enjoyable than traditional paper-and-pencil tests. Another advantage is that it models good instruction: students are assessed as they learn and learn as they are assessed.

Performance Assessment in *ScienceFusion*

Performance tasks can be found in two locations in *ScienceFusion*. In the Teacher Edition, a brief performance task is part of the information that accompanies each Review. In this Assessment Guide, a more comprehensive task follows each Unit Test as well as the "Safety in Science and Science Tools" section. Both types of performance tasks will provide insights into students' ability to apply key science inquiry skills and concepts taught in the unit.

Administering Performance Tasks

Unlike traditional assessment tools, performance assessment does not provide standardized directions for its administration or impose specific time limits on students, although a suggested time frame is offered as a guideline. The suggestions that follow may help you define your role in this assessment.

- **Be prepared.**
  A few days before students begin the task, read the Teacher's Directions and gather the materials needed.

- **Be clear.**
  Explain the directions for the task; rephrase them as needed. Also, explain how students' performance will be evaluated. Show students the rubric you plan to use, and explain the performance indicators in language your students understand.

- **Be encouraging.**
  Your role in administering the assessments should be that of a coach—motivating, guiding, and encouraging students to produce their best work.

- **Be supportive.**
  You may assist students who need help. The amount of assistance needed will depend on the needs and abilities of individual students.

- *Be flexible.*
  Not all students need to proceed through the performance task at the same rate and in the same manner. Allow students adequate time to do their best work.

- *Involve students in evaluation.*
  Invite students to join you as partners in the evaluation process, particularly in development or modification of the rubric.

Rubrics for Assessing Performance

A well-written rubric can help you score students' work accurately and fairly. Moreover, a rubric gives students a better idea before they begin a task of what qualities their work should exhibit.

Each performance task in the program has its own rubric. The rubric lists performance indicators, which are brief statements of what to look for in assessing the skills and understandings that the task addresses. A sample rubric for a task in this Assessment Guide follows.

Scoring Rubric

Performance Indicators

_____ Assembles the kite successfully.

_____ Carries out the experiment daily.

_____ Records results accurately.

_____ Makes an accurate chart and uses it to report the strength of wind observed each day.

Observations and Rubric Score

3	2	1	0

Scoring a Performance Task

The scoring system used for performance tasks in this Assessment Guide is a 4-point scale that is compatible with those used by many state assessment programs. You may wish to modify the rubrics as a 3- or 5-point scale. To determine a student's score on a performance task, review the indicators checked on the rubric and then select the score that best represents the student's overall performance on the task.

4-Point Scale			
Excellent Achievement	Adequate Achievement	Limited Achievement	Little or No Achievement
3	2	1	0

How to Convert a Rubric Score into a Grade

If, for grading purposes, you want to record a letter or numerical grade rather than a holistic score for the student's performance on a task, you can use the following conversion table.

Holistic Score	Letter Grade	Numerical Grade
3	A	90–100
2	B	80–89
1	C	70–79
0	D–F	69 or below

Developing Your Own Rubric

From time to time, you may want to either develop your own rubric or work together with your students to create one. Research has shown that significantly improved performance can result from student participation in the construction of rubrics.

Developing a rubric for a performance task involves three basic steps: (1) Identify the inquiry skills that are taught in the chapter and that students must perform to complete the task successfully, and identify what understanding of content is also required. (2) Determine which skills and understandings are involved in each step. (3) Decide what you will look for to confirm that students have acquired each skill and understanding you identified.

Classroom Observation

"Kid watching" is a natural part of teaching and an important part of evaluation. The purpose of classroom observation in assessment is to gather and record information that can lead to improved instruction. In this booklet, you will find an Observation Checklist (p. AG xv) on which you can record noteworthy observations of students' ability to use science inquiry skills.

Using the Observation Checklist

- *Identify the skills you will observe.*
  Find out which inquiry skills are introduced and reinforced in the chapter.

- *Focus on only a few students at a time.*
  You will find this more effective than trying to observe the entire class at once.

- *Look for a pattern.*
  It is important to observe a student's strengths and weaknesses over a period of time to determine whether a pattern exists.

- *Plan how and when to record observations.*
  Decide whether to

  —record observations immediately on the checklist as you move about the room or

  —make jottings or mental notes of observations and record them later.

- *Don't agonize over the ratings.*
  Students who stand out as particularly strong will clearly merit a rating of 3 ("Outstanding"). Others may clearly earn a rating of 1 ("Needs Improvement"). This doesn't mean, however, that a 2 ("Satisfactory") is automatically the appropriate rating for the rest of the class. For example, you may not have had sufficient opportunity to observe a student demonstrate certain skills. The checklist cells for these skills should remain blank under the student's name until you have observed him or her perform the skills.

- *Review your checklist periodically, and ask yourself questions such as these:*

  What are the student's strongest/weakest attributes?

  In what ways has the student shown growth?

  In what areas does the class as a whole show strength/weakness?

  What kinds of activities would encourage growth?

  Do I need to allot more time to classroom observation?

- *Use the data you collect.*
  Refer to your classroom observation checklists when you plan lessons, form groups, assign grades, and confer with students and family members.

Date _____

Rating Scale		
3 Outstanding	**1** Needs Improvement	
2 Satisfactory	☐ Not Enough Opportunity to Observe	

Names of Students

Inquiry Skills										
Observe										
Compare										
Classify/Order										
Gather, Record, Display, or Interpret Data										
Use Numbers										
Communicate										
Plan and Conduct Simple Investigations										
Measure										
Predict										
Infer										
Draw Conclusions										
Use Time/Space Relationships										
Hypothesize										
Formulate or Use Models										
Identify and Control Variables										
Experiment										

Using Student Self-Assessment

Researchers have evidence that self-evaluation and the reflection it involves can have positive effects on students' learning. To achieve these effects, students must be challenged to reflect on their work and to monitor, analyze, and control their own learning—beginning in the earliest grades.

Frequent opportunities for students to evaluate their performance build the skills and confidence they need for effective self-assessment. A trusting relationship between the student and the teacher is also essential. Students must be assured that honest responses can have only a positive effect on the teacher's view of them and that responses will not be used to determine grades.

Three checklists are found in this Assessment Guide. One is Self-Assessment—Active Reading: a form that leads students to reflect on and evaluate their role as active readers. The second is the Experiment/Project Summary Sheet: a form to help students describe and evaluate any projects or activities they may have designed or conducted as independent inquiry. The third is the Self-Assessment—My Science Notebook: a form to help students evaluate how well they use their student notebooks.

Using Self-Assessment Forms

- *Explain the directions.*
  Discuss the forms and how to complete them.

- *Encourage honest responses.*
  Be sure to tell students that there are no "right" responses to the items.

- *Model the process.*
  One way to foster candid responses is to model the process yourself, including at least one response that is not positive. Discuss reasons for your responses.

- *Be open to variations in students' responses.*
  Negative responses should not be viewed as indicating weaknesses. Rather, they confirm that you did a good job of communicating the importance of honesty in self-assessment.

- *Discuss responses with students.*
  You may wish to clarify students' responses in conferences with them and in family conferences. Invite both students and family members to help you plan activities for school and home that will motivate and support students' growth in science.

Think About It

To find out if you are an Active Reader, write "yes" if a sentence describes what you did when you read the lesson.

_____ 1. Every page or two, I stopped to think about what I had read to be sure I understood it.

_____ 2. I followed the Active Reading directions in each lesson.

_____ 3. When I did not understand something, I put a question mark in the margin so I would remember to ask about it.

_____ 4. I paused to study the photographs, diagrams, and charts on every page.

_____ 5. I recorded notes on the pages of my book to help me remember key ideas.

_____ 6. I used the Answer Key in Sum It Up and made sure all my answers were correct.

_____ 7. I used my notes and Active Reading marks as a study guide for tests.

This is how being an Active Reader helped me.

_____

_____

_____

_____

_____

This is what I will do to be a more Active Reader next time.

_____

_____

_____

_____

_____

Name _____

My Experiment/Project

You can tell about your science project or experiment by completing the following sentences.

1. My experiment/project was about _____
   _____
   _____

2. I worked on this experiment/project with _____
   _____
   _____

3. I gathered information from these sources: _____
   _____
   _____

4. The most important thing I learned from doing this experiment/project is _____
   _____
   _____

5. I think I did a (an) _____ job on my experiment/project because _____
   _____
   _____

6. I'd also like to tell you _____
   _____
   _____
   _____
   _____

Think About It

Do you keep a Science Notebook? Write "yes" if a sentence describes your Science Notebook.

_____ 1. I am building a table of contents in the first four pages of my notebook. I add entries throughout the year.

_____ 2. I am building an index in the back of my notebook. I add entries throughout the year.

_____ 3. I write my plans for investigations in my notebook. My plans include questions I want to investigate and the procedures I will follow.

_____ 4. I record results, notes, and data from my investigations.

_____ 5. I use my notebook to record science notes, drawings, and graphic organizers.

_____ 6. I include the date and a title with each entry in my notebook.

_____ 7. I use my notebook to review and reflect on what I have learned.

This is how keeping a Science Notebook is helping me.

_____

_____

_____

_____

_____

_____

This is what I will do to improve my Science Notebook.

_____

_____

_____

_____

_____

_____

_____

Portfolio Assessment

A portfolio is a showcase for student work, a place where many types of assignments, projects, reports, and writings can be collected. The work samples in the collection provide "snapshots" of the student's efforts over time, and taken together they reveal the student's growth, attitudes, and understanding better than any other type of assessment. However, portfolios are not ends in themselves. Their value comes from creating them, discussing them, and using them to improve learning.

The purpose of using portfolios in science is threefold:

- *To give the student a voice in the assessment process.*
- *To foster reflection, self-monitoring, and self-evaluation.*
- *To provide a comprehensive picture of a student's progress.*

Portfolio Assessment in *ScienceFusion*

In *ScienceFusion*, students may assemble portfolio collections of their work. The collection may include a few required papers, such as tests, performance tasks, lab response pages, and Experiment/Project Summary Sheets.

From time to time, consider including other measures (Science Experiences Record, Self-Assessment—Active Reading, Self-Assessment—My Science Notebook). The Science Experiences Record, for example, can reveal insights about student interests, ideas, and out-of-school experiences (museum visits, nature walks, outside readings, and so on) that otherwise you might not know about. Materials to help you and your students build portfolios and use them for evaluation are included in the pages that follow.

Using Portfolio Assessment

- *Explain the portfolio and its use.*
  Describe how people in many fields use portfolios to present samples of their work when they are applying for a job. Tell students that they can create their own portfolio to show what they have learned, what skills they have acquired, and how they think they are doing in science.

- *Decide what standard pieces should be included.*
  Encourage students to identify a few standard, or "required," work samples that they will include in their portfolios, and discuss reasons for including them. The Student Task sheets for the performance assessments in this Assessment Guide, for example, might be standard samples in the portfolios because they show students' ability to use inquiry skills and critical thinking skills. Together with your class, decide on the required work samples that everyone's portfolio will include.

- *Discuss student-selected work samples.*
  Point out that the best work to select is not necessarily the longest or the neatest. Rather, it is work the student believes will best demonstrate his or her growth in science understanding and skills.

- *Establish a basic plan.*
  Decide about how many work samples will be included in the portfolio and when they should be selected. Ask students to list on the Guide to My Science Portfolio (p. AG xxiii) each sample they select and to explain why they selected it.

- *Tell students how you will evaluate their portfolios.*
  Use a blank Portfolio Evaluation Checklist to explain how you will evaluate the contents of a portfolio.

- *Use the portfolio.*
  Use the portfolio as a handy reference tool in determining students' science grades and in holding conferences with them and family members. You may wish to send the portfolio home for family members to review.

Name _____

My Science Experiences

Date	What I Did	What I Thought or Learned

Name ______________________________

Guide to My Science Portfolio

My Science Portfolio

What Is in My Portfolio	Why I Chose It
1.	
2.	
3.	
4.	
5.	
6.	
7.	

I organized my Science Portfolio this way because ______________________________

____

____

____

____

____

Name _____ Date _____

Portfolio Evaluation

Aspects of Science Literacy	Evidence of Growth
1. **Understands science concepts** (*scientific investigation and reasoning; matter and energy; force, motion, and energy; Earth and space; organisms and environments*)	_____ _____ _____
2. **Uses inquiry skills** (*observes, compares, classifies, gathers/ interprets data, communicates, measures, experiments, infers, predicts, draws conclusions*)	_____ _____ _____
3. **Thinks critically** (*analyzes, synthesizes, evaluates, applies ideas effectively, solves problems*)	_____ _____ _____
4. **Displays traits/attitudes of a scientist** (*is curious, questioning, persistent, precise, creative, enthusiastic; uses science materials carefully; is concerned for environment*)	_____ _____ _____

Summary of Portfolio Assessment

For This Review			Since Last Review		
Excellent	Good	Fair	Improving	About the Same	Not as Good

Name _____ Date _____

Science Safety

❶ What is the purpose of the caution symbols shown in your science book and around the classroom laboratory space?

(A) The symbols divide the procedure into steps each group must complete while doing a classroom investigation.

(B) The symbols show which equipment you will need while doing a classroom investigation.

(C) The symbols identify which parts of your science book must be filled out while doing a classroom investigation.

(D) The symbols indicate which safety practices you must demonstrate while doing a classroom investigation.

❷ Which safe practice must you demonstrate as part of any outdoor laboratory investigation?

(A) You must always wear gloves while performing an investigation outdoors.

(B) You must always complete a data table as part of an outdoor investigation.

(C) You must always carry a fire extinguisher along during an outdoor investigation.

(D) You must always demonstrate appropriate safety practices during an outdoor investigation.

❸ Joyce sees the safety symbol below in her lab procedure. Which safety equipment must she use as part of the lab?

(A) gloves

(B) binoculars

(C) safety goggles

(D) reading glasses

❹ Why is it important to wear gloves when indicated in a lab investigation procedure?

(A) Gloves will help you to hold on to things.

(B) Gloves allow everyone to stay dry during the lab.

(C) Gloves can keep your hands away from chemicals, soil, or other substances that aren't safe to touch.

(D) Gloves will prevent you from getting cold during the lab.

❺ Which pieces of safety equipment should usually be worn for classroom lab investigations you do?

(A) apron and goggles

(B) goggles and helmet

(C) binoculars and apron

(D) helmet and binoculars

6 A group of students and their teacher are observing birds. Which piece of equipment should they bring along to demonstrate the use of safety equipment during outdoor investigations?

(A) a cell phone

(B) a camping ax

(C) a first-aid kit

(D) a fire extinguisher

7 Which type of footwear should you avoid wearing in a science laboratory?

(A) boots   (C) sandals

(B) loafers   (D) sneakers

8 Where is the proper place to dispose of broken glass?

(A) desk   (C) outside

(B) sink drain   (D) trashcan

9 During a classroom investigation, you notice that the lab procedure indicates that some items you will use are poisonous. What safety precaution should you take?

(A) do not touch anything

(B) keep a fire extinguisher nearby

(C) keep long hair pulled back

(D) do not put anything in your mouth

10 Which activity is permitted in a science lab because it demonstrates a safe practice during a classroom investigation?

(A) eating food

(B) chewing gum

(C) washing hands

(D) applying makeup

11 Which item would you most likely find in the box shown below?

(A) snacks

(B) pencils

(C) goggles

(D) bandages

12 Which piece of safety equipment can be used to protect your eyes from hazards in a science lab?

(A) lab aprons

(B) metal tongs

(C) rubber gloves

(D) safety goggles

13 The investigation you are performing includes working with chemicals. What safety precaution should you take?

(A) You should drink plenty of water during the investigation.

(B) You should remove your eyeglasses during the investigation.

(C) You should keep a beaker of water on your desk during the investigation.

(D) You should wear gloves and goggles during the investigation.

14 Which of the following hazards can be dealt with safely by wearing gloves in the classroom laboratory?

(A) fire   (C) fumes

(B) spills   (D) electricity

15 You are working with a partner doing an investigation outside in which the two of you are observing plants. Which safety rule should you both keep in mind?

(A) avoid touching the plants with your hands

(B) keep a fire extinguisher with you at all times

(C) take turns picking the plants and collecting them

(D) throw the plants in the trash when you are done with them

16 What should you do if the fire alarm sounds while you are performing a scientific investigation in the classroom?

(A) listen to your teacher and leave the classroom immediately

(B) gather your science materials to take with you to another location

(C) finish the experiment as quickly as possible

(D) ignore the fire alarm until you know for sure there is a fire

17 What should you do to prepare for a science investigation if you know that you will be working with fire or an open flame?

(A) You should tie your hair back.

(B) You should put on a gas mask.

(C) You should put on rubber gloves.

(D) You should dress in warm clothing.

18 What is the safest way to unplug an electric appliance from an outlet?

(A) pull quickly on the cord

(B) hold the cord and wiggle it slowly

(C) grip the plug and pull slowly

(D) use your foot to push the plug away

Name _____ Date _____

19 Which type of gloves is best for handling things that are very hot?

(A) thin plastic gloves

(B) loose rubber gloves

(C) thick insulated gloves

(D) comfortable cotton gloves

20 You are getting ready to perform a lab investigation in which you will heat chemicals. Your teacher asks you to put on safety goggles during the lab. What should you do if you wear eyeglasses?

(A) You must remove your eyeglasses during the lab.

(B) You should wear the goggles over your eyeglasses.

(C) You should wear your eyeglasses over your safety goggles.

(D) You do not need to wear safety goggles because the eyeglasses will protect your eyes.

21 You are performing a lab procedure that calls for mixing several chemicals. You cannot find one of the chemicals that you need in your supplies. What should you do?

(A) You should stop working in the lab.

(B) You should ask your teacher for the chemical.

(C) You should look for a similar chemical and use it.

(D) You should mix the other chemicals and leave that one out.

22 Your class is performing an investigation outdoors. Which areas can you go into as part of the investigation?

(A) You can go anywhere that you see other students.

(B) You will need to stay on sidewalks during the investigation.

(C) You must ask your teacher to define the boundaries for your investigation.

(D) You should only go as far from the school as you need to in order to collect data.

23 What should you do during an investigation if you are wearing a shirt with long sleeves?

(A) make sure your sleeves are buttoned at the wrist

(B) roll up your sleeves to keep them away from materials

(C) change your shirt before the investigation

(D) put on a sweater over your shirt before the investigation

24 What should you do if you spill a chemical during an investigation?

(A) wipe up the chemical with a paper towel

(B) leave the chemical and observe it for several minutes

(C) stop working immediately and notify your teacher

(D) look up the chemical in your textbook to find out if it is dangerous or not

Write the answers to these questions.

25 Describe the location of the fire extinguisher in your classroom and explain how it is used.

_____

_____

26 Look at the picture. Which pieces of safety equipment are being used in the picture? How are they being used?

_____

_____

27 Your classmate has long hair that she ties back before doing a lab experiment. Explain why this is a good safety practice.

_____

_____

28 What safety practices should you keep in mind if you are working with living creatures during an outdoor investigation?

_____

_____

29 Describe the proper way to wash your hands following a lab experiment.

_____

_____

_____

30 What should you do if you are unsure of how to use a piece of lab equipment during a lab investigation?

_____

_____

Science Tools

1 You and your classmates are planning an investigation that involves watching plants grow over a period of time and then describing what you observed. Which equipment might you select to collect data with as you implement this investigation?

- (A) a stopwatch
- (B) a thermometer
- (C) a digital camera
- (D) a graduated cylinder

2 Your teacher asks you to plan an investigation in which you will observe and record the temperature outside of your house for a week. Which piece of equipment would you use to implement this investigation?

- (A) a telescope
- (B) a windsock
- (C) a rain gauge
- (D) a thermometer

3 You can use current technology to construct a simple table like the one below to organize data so that others can easily understand the information. In which two ways are the data organized?

	Car 1	Car 2	Car 3
Time	1:23	1:44	1:06

- (A) The data are organized according to different cars and races.
- (B) The data are organized according to different days and times.
- (C) The data are organized according to different races and days.
- (D) The data are organized according to different times and cars.

4 To organize, examine, and evaluate her data, Tamara has used current technology as a tool to construct the graphic below. In what form are the data organized?

Animals	Owl	Dog	Horse
Eats meat?	yes	yes	no
Lays eggs?	yes	no	no
Fur?	no	yes	yes

- (A) a map
- (B) a chart
- (C) a data table
- (D) a bar graph

5 Observations from a scientific investigation can be organized in ways that allow them to be examined and evaluated quickly. The data listed below were compiled using current technology. In what form is the information below organized?

	Plant A	Plant B
Height	14 cm	16 cm
Mass	22 g	18 g

- (A) a bar graph
- (B) a data table
- (C) a flow chart
- (D) a research map

6 You are planning to find the average height of students in each grade at your school. Which tool might you use to collect and record this information?

- (A) a scale
- (B) a camera
- (C) a calculator
- (D) a microscope

7 Dr. Thomas collected data about rainfall in four types of forests. She constructed the bar graph below using current technology to examine and evaluate her data. Which forest gets the most rainfall each year on average?

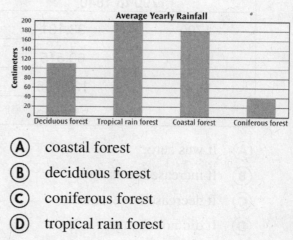

- (A) coastal forest
- (B) deciduous forest
- (C) coniferous forest
- (D) tropical rain forest

8 Use the metric ruler shown below to measure the crayon and collect data in the form of millimeters.

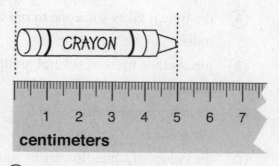

- (A) The crayon is 5 mm long.
- (B) The crayon is 50 mm long.
- (C) The crayon is 500 mm long.
- (D) The crayon is 5,000 mm long.

Name _____ Date _____

9 The chart below was made using current technology. Examine and evaluate the data presented in it. What do the data say about the size of the population being studied?

New York City's Population, 1790 to 1840	
1790	33,131
1800	60,515
1820	123,706
1840	312,710

(A) It was zero.

(B) It increased over time.

(C) It decreased over time.

(D) It did not change.

10 You would use a calculator as a tool to analyze which of the following sets of information?

(A) the time it takes someone to run a mile

(B) the average mass of several groups of rocks

(C) the temperature inside your classroom

(D) the colors of some flowers in your schoolyard

11 Which type of tool might you use if you wanted to collect and record images of different bird species?

(A) a scale   (C) a calculator

(B) a camera   (D) a thermometer

12 Scientists can use current technology to organize data in many different ways. Which method of organizing scientific data is shown below?

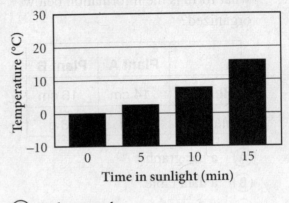

Change in Water Temperature

(A) a bar graph

(B) a line graph

(C) a circle graph

(D) a square diagram

13 Your teacher has constructed the map below to organize, examine, and evaluate information about your school playground. What type of information does this map give you?

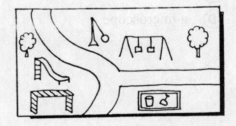

(A) It shows how close the bus stop is to the playground.

(B) It shows where the playground is located in the city.

(C) It shows where each piece of equipment is located in relation to the other pieces.

(D) It shows the distance in meters between each piece of equipment.

14 You are using a mirror to collect and analyze information about light. What happens to light when it hits a mirror?

(A) Light is emitted by a mirror.

(B) Light is distorted by a mirror.

(C) Light is absorbed by a mirror.

(D) Light is reflected by a mirror.

15 The map shown below allows you to examine and evaluate which type of data about the different locations?

(A) the name of each country

(B) how far apart the countries are

(C) the names of the cities in each country

(D) which direction to travel to get from one country to another

16 How does a hand lens help you collect and analyze information?

(A) It allows you to see things that are far away.

(B) It captures an image of something on film.

(C) It helps you to see things when it is very dark.

(D) It makes it easier to see things that are small.

17 For what type of investigation might you use the tool shown below to collect and analyze information?

(A) to look at planets

(B) to measure rainfall

(C) to observe bacteria

(D) to track thunderstorms

18 Which organism could you analyze by observing it in an aquarium habitat?

(A) a fox   (C) a deer

(B) a bird   (D) a snail

19 How does using a computer as a tool to collect, record, and analyze information compare with working with a notebook and a pencil?

(A) The computer does the work much slower than you can do it with a notebook and pencil.

(B) The computer does the work much faster than you can do it with a notebook and pencil.

(C) The computer makes it easier for you to come up with ideas than if you use a notebook and pencil.

(D) The computer makes it harder for you to come up with ideas than if you use a notebook and pencil.

20 Which scientific tool is used to collect and analyze information about mass?

(A) a metric ruler

(B) a graduated cylinder

(C) a digital thermometer

(D) a triple-beam balance

21 The thermometer below was used to collect and record temperature data. What is the temperature in degrees Celsius?

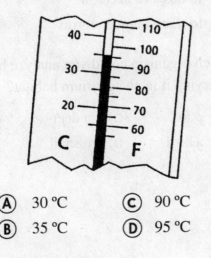

(A) 30 °C   (C) 90 °C

(B) 35 °C   (D) 95 °C

22 The spring scale shown below is a tool used to collect information for what type of measurement?

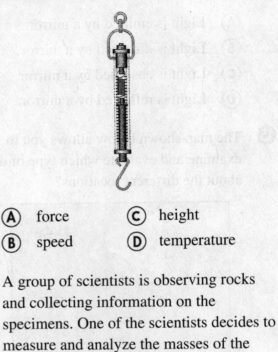

(A) force   (C) height

(B) speed   (D) temperature

23 A group of scientists is observing rocks and collecting information on the specimens. One of the scientists decides to measure and analyze the masses of the samples. Which tool should he use?

(A) a rain gauge

(B) a metric ruler

(C) a pan balance

(D) a digital thermometer

24 Why are binoculars a valuable tool for collecting information when observing organisms such as birds?

(A) Binoculars allow you to observe birds in a cage.

(B) Binoculars allow you to study birds in their natural habitat.

(C) Binoculars allow you to remain in the lab while you study birds.

(D) Binoculars allow you to examine microscopic features on birds.

25 Which tool should you always have with you to record and analyze information, no matter what you are studying or where you are doing an investigation?

(A) a collecting net

(B) a notebook

(C) a microscope

(D) a thermometer

26 Weather scientists in Crystal Falls use current technology to organize data into charts and graphs. Examine the bar graph below and evaluate the data about snowstorms. Which year had less snow than the rest?

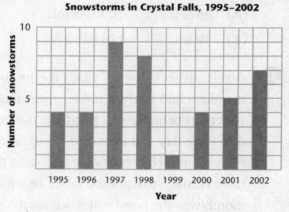

Snowstorms in Crystal Falls, 1995–2002

(A) 1997

(B) 1999

(C) 2000

(D) 2002

27 The chart below examines the state of a substance as it changes from solid to liquid to gas. What current technology was probably used to measure and collect the data for evaluation?

	Temperature	Heat energy
Solid	lowest	least
Liquid		
Gas	highest	most

(A) a laser ruler

(B) a satellite dish

(C) a solar battery

(D) a digital thermometer

28 You run a magnet through a group of small objects to collect and analyze information about their properties. Some of the objects stick to the magnet. What can you conclude about those objects?

(A) The objects are probably hot.

(B) The objects are probably cold.

(C) The objects are probably made of metal.

(D) The objects are probably made of stone.

Name _____ Date _____

29 Danielle has to record information in her notebook by hand. She must then use a calculator to analyze the data and then record the results. Which computer program could do this work for her more easily?

Ⓐ a photo editor

Ⓑ a web browser

Ⓒ a word processor

Ⓓ a spreadsheet program

30 Look at the data organized below. Which tool was likely used to collect and analyze this information?

Sample	Length (cm)
A	4.6
B	3.3
C	4.0
D	4.2
E	3.9

Ⓐ a metric ruler

Ⓑ a graduated cylinder

Ⓒ a triple-beam balance

Ⓓ a Celsius thermometer

31 A camper is walking through the woods. Which tool can she use to collect and analyze information about the direction in which she is walking?

Ⓐ a beaker

Ⓑ a compass

Ⓒ a meterstick

Ⓓ a spring scale

32 A teacher used graduated cylinders to collect and analyze information about the volume of rocks. She put 40 mL of liquid into the graduated cylinder on the left. She then placed a rock and 40 mL of liquid into the graduated cylinder on the right. The volume of the liquid and rock in that cylinder reads 75 mL. Analyze the results in the picture below. What is the volume of the rock?

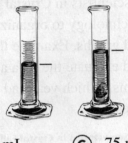

Ⓐ 35 mL   Ⓒ 75 mL

Ⓑ 40 mL   Ⓓ 115 mL

33 A scientist is using a Celsius thermometer to collect and analyze information about water temperature in a pond. He collected data each day and averaged the data for each month. His results are shown in the table below. Analyze the table. In which month was the pond water warmest?

Month	Temperature (°C)
September	20
October	23
November	16
December	8

Ⓐ September

Ⓑ October

Ⓒ November

Ⓓ December

34 You and your family are going on a camping trip. You would like to observe some birds during your trip and bring information back home to study. Which tool would help you collect and analyze your observations?

Ⓐ a hand lens

Ⓑ a stopwatch

Ⓒ a microscope

Ⓓ a digital camera

35 You can use the spring scale shown below to collect and analyze information about your textbook. If the scale reads 10, what can you conclude about the book?

Ⓐ The book has a weight of 10 N.

Ⓑ The book has a volume of 10 mL.

Ⓒ The book has a length of 10 mm.

Ⓓ The book has a temperature of 10 °C.

36 Which of the following tools can be used to collect and analyze information about the volume of a liquid in the laboratory?

Ⓐ a ruler

Ⓑ a beaker

Ⓒ a balance

Ⓓ a stopwatch

37 Your classmate is using the tool shown below to collect and analyze information as part of a lab. Why is she using this tool?

Ⓐ to mix a substance in the beaker

Ⓑ to heat a substance in the beaker

Ⓒ to freeze a substance in the beaker

Ⓓ to measure a substance in the beaker

38 Which tool would you use to record the amount of time it takes for a mouse to get through different types of mazes?

Ⓐ a computer   Ⓒ a meterstick

Ⓑ a stopwatch   Ⓓ a tape measure

39 The student shown below is measuring the height that a ball bounces. Which tool is she using to collect and analyze this information?

Ⓐ a meterstick

Ⓑ a metric ruler

Ⓒ a pan balance

Ⓓ a spring scale

Write the answers to these questions.

40 Complete the table below to examine and evaluate data about windstorms in two cities: Amarillo and Austin. On Monday, wind speeds in Amarillo were 12 kph, and wind speeds in Austin were 15 kph. Wind speeds were 5 kph on Tuesday in Austin, and they were 22 kph on Wednesday. On Tuesday, wind speeds were recorded at 16 kph in Amarillo. The wind speed for Amarillo on Wednesday was 2 kph, and on Thursday it was 9 kph. The wind speed in Austin on Thursday was 5 kph.

City	Monday wind	Tuesday wind	Wednesday wind	Thursday wind

41 Describe an investigation you could perform that would involve collecting and analyzing information with the help of a collecting net.

_____

_____

42 You are performing an investigation in which you must watch the clock and collect temperature readings from a solution every two hours and analyze them. You must take a total of four readings. If you start the procedure at 9 a.m., at what times must you take readings?

_____

43 You are using a stopwatch to time runners. You collect and record their times in your notebook. One runner runs 1 kilometer in 2 minutes. To analyze this information, calculate his running time in kilometers per hour.

_____

_____

Name ______________________________ Date __________

44 Describe one way that a pan balance and a triple-beam balance can be used to analyze data. How are they alike? Then describe one way they are different.

____

____

____

45 Why is it important to keep a science notebook while performing investigations?

____

____

Name _____ Date _____

Using Science Tools

Materials

paper, pencil

Procedure

❶ The list below includes common science tools. Each tool can be used to collect, record, and analyze scientific information.

calculator	spring scale	magnet
microscope	pan balance	collecting net
camera	triple-beam balance	notebook
computer	graduated cylinder	clock
hand lens	beaker	stopwatch
metric ruler	hot plate	terrarium
Celsius thermometer	meterstick	aquarium
mirror	compass	

❷ Read through the list and consider each of the tools. Think about how each tool is used in a scientific investigation. Construct a chart with information that explains how each tool is used to collect, record, and analyze information. Be as descriptive as possible.

Tool	Collect	Record	Analyze
calculator			
microscope			

Name _____ Date _____

Using Science Tools

Materials Performance Task sheets, paper or notebook, pencils

Time 40 minutes

Suggested Grouping individuals

Inquiry Skills identify, describe, compare, record information, communicate

Preparation Hints You may wish to use this exercise following one of the first classes in which you show students where equipment is located and how to use equipment. Ask students to look over the list of tools ahead of time and bring forward any questions they might have about the tools. Be prepared to demonstrate the use of any tools as necessary.

Introduce the Task Ask the students to think about the many different tools that scientists use to learn about science. Show students the list of tools and ask them to think about how these tools are used in science. Tell them that they will construct a chart to describe the different ways that tools are used.

Promote Discussion Extend the exercise by asking the students to think of other tools that scientists use. Have them list some of the tools they thought of and include descriptions of their uses.

Scoring Rubric

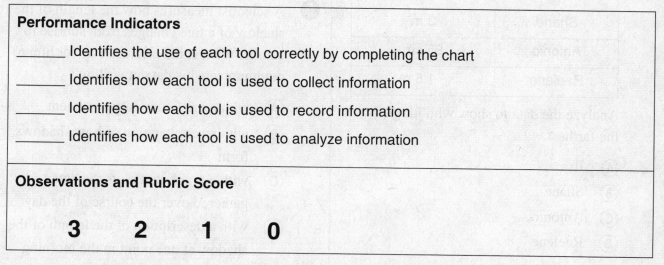

Performance Indicators

_____ Identifies the use of each tool correctly by completing the chart

_____ Identifies how each tool is used to collect information

_____ Identifies how each tool is used to record information

_____ Identifies how each tool is used to analyze information

Observations and Rubric Score

3   2   1   0

What Do Scientists Do?

1 A scientist says that most cats prefer chicken-based cat food. Jeremy wants to find out which cat food his cat likes best. How could he use observational testing to find out?

(A) observe and analyze his cat's reaction to different foods

(B) observe cat food commercials and analyze the messages

(C) observe and analyze which cat foods sell most quickly at the grocery store

(D) observe and analyze the behavior of cats on an animal program on television

2 Four members of the track team practice the long jump. Each jumper has a friend measure the length of the jump. The measurements are recorded below.

Jumper	Distance
Ilsa	82 cm
Shane	3 m
Antonio	95 cm
Raelene	1.5 m

Analyze the data to show who jumped the farthest.

(A) Ilsa

(B) Shane

(C) Antonio

(D) Raelene

3 Mrs. Davis wants students to be able to observe a toad's habitat so they can collect information over time. Which tool would be most helpful in making a classroom habitat?

(A) net

(B) beaker

(C) hand lens

(D) terrarium

4 Natalia has entered a paper airplane competition. She is planning to investigate which type of paper to use for her plane. Which is a well-defined question she should ask to guide her investigation?

(A) Which type of paper is the lightest?

(B) Which type of paper is the heaviest?

(C) Which wing style glides the farthest?

(D) Which type of paper makes a plane that glides the farthest?

5 A scientist measures how the length of the shadow of a tree changes from sunrise to sunset. What is the clearest way for him to communicate his data in writing?

(A) with a brief summary statement

(B) with an explanation of how shadows form

(C) with a graph that plots the data gathered over the course of the day

(D) with a description of the length of the shadow at one point in the morning and one point in the afternoon

Name _____ Date _____

What Skills Do Scientists Use?

❶ Jamal plans an investigation to test the strength of a packing foam material. He finds that the material gets a dent when he puts more than three bricks on it. What inference can he make?

Ⓐ The foam is very strong.

Ⓑ The bricks are too heavy for the test.

Ⓒ The foam will dent if he places six bricks on it.

Ⓓ The foam will lay flat if he places five blocks of wood on it.

❷ Which tool could you use to collect information on how much time it takes for the dye to be absorbed by a stalk of celery placed in a glass of red dye?

Ⓐ clock

Ⓑ hand lens

Ⓒ calculator

Ⓓ Celsius thermometer

❸ Reva wanted to determine if watering plants makes a difference in their growth. During her investigation, she watered only one of two plants. After a few days, she noticed that the plants looked different. How did she collect data?

Ⓐ by predicting

Ⓑ by observing

Ⓒ by measuring

Ⓓ by communicating

❹ Millions of honeybees have vanished from their hives throughout the country recently. Scientists have suggested several possible explanations, but no one is certain why this is happening. What do bee experts need to do to evaluate the different explanations?

Ⓐ talk about one of the explanations for a long time

Ⓑ examine all sides of the evidence presented by the scientists

Ⓒ decide to study the problem further after discarding one of the ideas

Ⓓ pick the best idea and apply it to the problem of a reduced bee population

❺ Sarah is taking part in an experiment on how quickly mold forms on bread. Which of these tools can she use to record the information she has collected?

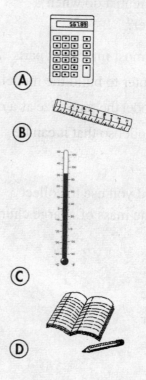

Ⓐ

Ⓑ

Ⓒ

Ⓓ

How Do Scientists Collect and Use Data?

1 Dr. Omar wants to use the metric system to collect data on the boy's illness. What unit of measure should he use to record the boy's temperature?

- Ⓐ grams
- Ⓑ degrees Celsius
- Ⓒ degrees Fahrenheit
- Ⓓ centimeters

2 A scientist plans to use a model to represent the natural world of a river. What must the scientist do when building the model?

- Ⓐ include the most important parts
- Ⓑ use a computer to build the model
- Ⓒ build the model the same size as a river
- Ⓓ build the model so that it can be taken apart

3 Which tool would you use to collect information on the mass of a large chunk of quartz?

- Ⓐ microscope
- Ⓑ spring scale
- Ⓒ metric ruler
- Ⓓ pan balance

4 Ricardo collects data on the time it takes six different types of caterpillars to turn into butterflies. He wants to construct a simple table to examine his data. Which pieces of data should he include when constructing the table?

- Ⓐ number of caterpillars and their location
- Ⓑ types of caterpillars and their location
- Ⓒ types of caterpillars and the number of days it took for butterflies to form
- Ⓓ number of caterpillars and the number of days it took for butterflies to form

5 Chloe measured the temperature and humidity every afternoon for four days. She recorded the results in the table below.

Day	Temperature (°C)	Humidity (%)
Monday	28	90
Tuesday	27	79
Wednesday	25	70
Thursday	28	69

Analyze the data. Which day was the most hot and humid?

- Ⓐ Monday
- Ⓑ Tuesday
- Ⓒ Wednesday
- Ⓓ Thursday

Why Do Scientists Compare Results?

❶ Devon, Margarita, Renee, and Malik implement an investigation after making muffins. They wonder whose muffins have the greatest diameter. Devon measures the diameter of his muffins with a meterstick. Margarita places jellybeans end to end. Renee uses coins, and Malik uses paper clips. Which student selected the appropriate tool to determine the diameter with the most accuracy?

Ⓐ Malik

Ⓑ Devon

Ⓒ Renee

Ⓓ Margarita

❷ Jessica is studying the parts of a plant. Which tool should she use to implement an investigation on the structure of a leaf?

Ⓐ hand lens

Ⓑ telescope

Ⓒ computer

Ⓓ meterstick

❸ Why would a scientist use a spring scale to collect information?

Ⓐ to find the mass of something

Ⓑ to find the length of something

Ⓒ to find the weight of something

Ⓓ to find the volume of something

❹ Sasha is tracking the growth of three bean plants planted in three different types of soil. Each week, she uses a meterstick to measure each plant's growth. She wants to construct a table to organize the data she is collecting. What should she write in the first column of the table below?

	Plant 1	Plant 2	Plant 3

Ⓐ Soil 1, Soil 2, Soil 3

Ⓑ Test 1, Test 2, Test 3

Ⓒ Bean 1, Bean 2, Bean 3

Ⓓ Week 1, Week 2, Week 3

❺ Tomás collects data on the amount of time it takes for sunflowers to turn toward the sun. Which would be the best way to record the data?

Ⓐ numerals

Ⓑ concept maps

Ⓒ labeled drawings

Ⓓ descriptive words

What Kinds of Models Do Scientists Use?

1 Hiroto wonders about the changes that take place as a tadpole grows into a frog. What type of model would be most useful for representing how tadpoles change into frogs in the natural world?

(A) plastic models of two different types of frogs

(B) a computer animation of the life cycle of a frog

(C) a diagram that shows the different parts of a frog's body

(D) photographs of a tadpole and a fully grown frog

2 Lukas wants to make a model of the river shown below. What is one limitation the model will have in representing the natural world?

(A) It will not be able to show the forest.

(B) It will not be able to show the shoreline.

(C) It will not be able to show people using the river.

(D) It will not be able to show the actual size of the river.

3 Scientists use different models depending on the subject they are studying. What is true about all models that represent the natural world?

(A) They help humans understand nature.

(B) They represent one object in nature at a time.

(C) They are the same size as the objects in nature.

(D) They include every detail of the objects that are in nature.

4 Vanessa reads that a bird's bones are hollow but strong. Vanessa wants to build a 3-D model of a bird. Which material would be her best choice to use for bones in her model?

(A) toothpicks   (C) blades of grass

(B) modeling clay   (D) drinking straws

5 Ida wants to build a 3-D model based on a complete fossil of an extinct bird. What is one limitation in accuracy that she will face as she works to represent the natural world of the bird?

(A) representing the size of the bird

(B) representing the shape of the bird

(C) representing the colors of the bird

(D) representing the bones of the bird

How Can You Model a School?

❶ Two students include metersticks, screwdrivers, and calculators when planning how to make a model. How can they group these objects?

(A) as tools

(C) as systems

(B) as designs

(D) as processes

❷ Jayden used measurements taken with a meterstick to make a 2-D model of the length and width of his classroom. Which of the following shows a limitation in the accuracy of the model?

(A) The model is too large to be useful.

(B) The model lacks information about the floor of the classroom.

(C) The model lacks information about the walls of the classroom.

(D) The model lacks information about the length and width of the classroom.

❸ Diya wants to make a classroom model of the solar system. What is one limitation the model will have?

(A) the inability to show all the planets

(B) the inability to show the size of the solar system

(C) the inability to show how the planets orbit around the sun

(D) the inability to show which planets are farthest from the sun

❹ Four students write an explanation of a 3-D model of their classroom. Their goal is to help people understand how much total space there is in the classroom. Which of the following descriptions accomplishes the goal?

(A) The classroom measures 5 m by 5 m.

(B) The six classroom windows measure 1 m by 1.5 m.

(C) The classroom is 5 m long and 9 m high.

(D) The floor plan measures 5 m by 5 m, and the height is 9 m.

❺ Kayla has made a model of her classroom. She says that the length of the classroom is twice the height of the ceiling in her model. How could she determine if the model is accurate?

(A) She could compare her model with another student's model.

(B) She could use a meterstick to measure the length and width of the classroom.

(C) She could use a meterstick to measure the height of each desk in the classroom.

(D) She could use a meterstick to measure the length and height of the classroom.

Studying Science

TEKS DOK Skill Builder

Use the following practice questions to help students build their comprehension skills for one TEKS at increasing depths of knowledge. The teacher notes below provide answers and strategies for diagnosing incorrect responses.

4.2A

Level 1: Recall and Reproduction

1. B; A pan balance measures mass. **Diagnose:** Ask students to identify what each answer choice measures. Students who miss this question might not recall that scientists use a meterstick to measure length, a pan balance to measure mass, a spring scale to measure force, and a thermometer to measure temperature. Have students who miss this question use the Student Edition or digital lesson to review what each tool measures. If students chose answer C, remind them of the difference between mass and force.

Level 2: Skills and Concepts

2. A; A pan balance measures mass, so Jessica is asking which object has the greater mass. **Diagnose:** Ask students what the pictures show. If they say that the pictures show a spoon and toy car on a pan balance, ask what a pan balance measures. Students who miss this question should review the discussion of pan balances in the Student Edition or digital lesson.

Level 3: Strategic Thinking

3. D; Sam used a pan balance and a graduated cylinder to collect data. **Diagnose:** Ask students what the graphs show. Then ask how scientists measure mass and volume. If they do not recall how mass and volume are measured, have them review the discussion of tools in the Student Edition or digital lesson.

Studying Science

Choose the letter of the best answer.

TEKS 4.2A

1 Manuel is planning a descriptive investigation to find which rock in his collection has the largest mass. Which equipment should he choose to answer his question?

- (A) meterstick
- (B) pan balance
- (C) spring scale
- (D) thermometer

2 Jessica is using the following piece of equipment in her descriptive investigation.

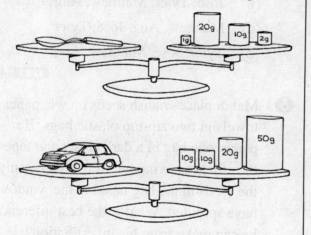

What well-defined question is she asking?

- (A) Which object has the greater mass?
- (B) Which object has the greater force?
- (C) Which object has the greater length?
- (D) Which object has the greater volume?

3 Sam created the graphs below to report the findings of his descriptive investigation.

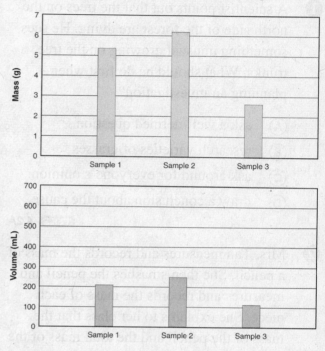

Based on the graphs, what inference can you make about the equipment Sam used in his investigation?

- (A) He used a spring scale and a pan balance.
- (B) He used a triple-beam balance and a meterstick.
- (C) He used a graduated cylinder and a spring balance.
- (D) He used a pan balance and a graduated cylinder.

Studying Science

Vocabulary and Concepts

1 A scientist points out that the trees on the north side of the forest are dying. He sees something unusual growing on the tree trunks. What should he do first when planning an investigation?

(A) ask a well-defined question

(B) research varieties of grasses

(C) ask around for everyone's opinion

(D) draw a conclusion about the cause

TEKS 4.2A

2 Mrs. Tan measures and records the mass of a pencil. She then smashes the pencil and measures and records the mass of each piece. She explains to her class that the mass of the pencil and the total mass of the pieces will be the same. How could her students evaluate this explanation?

(A) obtain the mass of another pencil

(B) verify the material used to make the pencil

(C) smash three more pencils to see how easily they break

(D) examine the scientific evidence that led to the explanation

TEKS 4.3A

3 Which tool would a scientist use to measure the weight of a book?

(A) a meterstick

(B) a pan balance

(C) a spring scale

(D) a triple beam balance

TEKS 4.4A

4 The table below shows the finishing times for a race.

Student	Time (sec)
Ang	85.32
José	80.09
Tyler	78.89
Matthew	80.15

Interpret the pattern to explain the correct finishing order from fastest to slowest.

(A) Ang, Matthew, Tyler, José

(B) José, Tyler, Matthew, Ang

(C) Matthew, Ang, José, Tyler

(D) Tyler, José, Matthew, Ang

TEKS 4.2D

5 Mahdi places radish seeds on wet paper towels in two zip-top plastic bags. He places one bag in a dark closet and tapes the other to a window. In five days, only the seeds in the bag taped to the window have sprouted. What is the best inference he can make from his investigation?

(A) Seeds need air to grow.

(B) Seeds need light to grow.

(C) Seeds need water to grow.

(D) Not all radish seeds sprout.

TEKS 4.2A

6 Anne is asked to use a model to represent the natural world. She uses an apple to represent Earth's layers. What is the most serious limitation of this model?

(A) the fact that it can be eaten

(B) the fact that it is two-dimensional

(C) the fact that its size is not accurate

(D) the fact that it is three-dimensional

TEKS 4.3C

7 Leon used clay to construct a model of a small fossil. A drawing of his model is shown below.

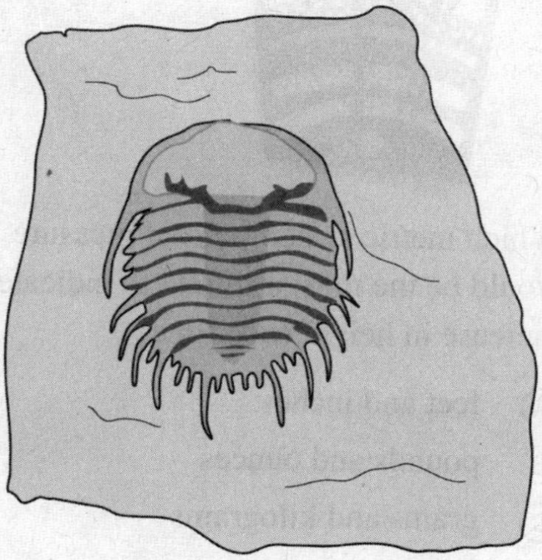

What is the most important limitation Leon should consider when evaluating the accuracy of his model?

(A) age of the fossil

(B) color of the clay

(C) texture of the fossil

(D) structure of the fossil

TEKS 4.3C

8 A student wants to bounce light from a flashlight onto a wall. Which tool could she use?

(A) mirror

(B) camera

(C) hand lens

(D) collecting net

TEKS 4.4A

9 Tereza plans an experiment investigating the effect of darkness on plant growth. She uses three similar plants that are planted in the same type of soil. All are given the same amount of water. One plant is placed in the dark. One plant is placed in a lighted terrarium. One plant is placed in full sun. She measures the growth of the plants each week for three weeks. She decides to create a table like the one below to examine her data.

Week 1			
Week 2			
Week 3			

What should Tereza add to the three columns in row 1?

(A) Water, Light, Soil

(B) Soil 1, Soil 2, Soil 3

(C) Water 1, Water 2, Water 3

(D) Darkness, Terrarium, Full Sun

TEKS 4.2C

10 A scientist needs to compare the exact mass of three different objects that are very similar. Which tool should she use?

(A) spring scale

(B) pan balance

(C) triple beam balance

(D) graduated cylinders

TEKS 4.4A

11 Four classmates measure the mass of the same sample of rock salt. When collecting data using the metric system, which measurement is the most precise?

(A) 1 kg

(B) 0.89 kg

(C) 0.90 kg

(D) 0.8937 kg

TEKS 4.2B

12 A scientist picks tomatoes from his garden. He carefully records the date and number of tomatoes he picks. He also wants to record the condition of each tomato. Which tool could he use to record the condition of each tomato?

(A) camera

(B) computer

(C) pan balance

(D) collecting net

TEKS 4.4A

13 Liam is in charge of recording the bar height cleared by three athletes attempting to set a new pole-vaulting record. The bar is raised a very small amount with each jump.

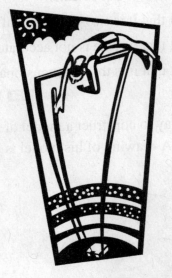

Which metric system unit of measure would be the most accurate to indicate the increase in height each time?

(A) feet and inches

(B) pounds and ounces

(C) grams and kilograms

(D) meters and centimeters

TEKS 4.2B

14 A team of students works on a class project. The students want to use craft sticks to build a bridge that can hold a 5 kg mass without breaking. They want to investigate several different designs before actually building the bridge. Which form of technology should they select for their investigation?

(A) computer

(B) hand lens

(C) microscope

(D) triple beam balance

TEKS 4.2A

15 Maya is studying two types of fish for a project. She draws pictures of the fish.

Clownfish   Boxfish

She also wants to use descriptive words to record her data. Which description would be most helpful as a record of her data?

(A) The boxfish has a funny shape.

(B) Most people have seen pictures of clownfish.

(C) The clownfish has stripes around its head, body, and tail.

(D) People will laugh when they see the picture of the boxfish.

TEKS 4.2B

16 A scientist is studying the feeding behavior of the American goldfinch. He is aware that the bird likes thistle seed. The scientist places three test feeders. Each feeder contains a different quality of thistle seed. The scientist records the number of birds on each feeder over a 2-hour period. How did the scientist collect his data?

(A) by inferring

(B) by observing

(C) by predicting

(D) by communicating

TEKS 4.2B

17 Which tool would be best for collecting information about the number of bacteria in a sample of water?

(A) telescope

(B) hand lens

(C) microscope

(D) collecting net

TEKS 4.4A

18 Riko collects one leaf from each tree around the school. What would be the best way for her to find out which leaf has the greatest mass?

(A) Hold the leaves, two at a time, in her hands.

(B) Find the mass of each leaf in a pan balance.

(C) Hang all of the leaves together from a spring scale.

(D) Lay each leaf on a table beside a measuring tape.

TEKS 4.4A

Apply Inquiry and Review the Big Ideas
Write the answers to these questions.

19 Fran investigates how a river flowing down a mountain washes away sand, dirt, and soil. Fran builds a pile of sand that resembles a mountain. She observes what happens when she pours a stream of water on the sand pile. Explain how Fran used a model to investigate the natural world and why she would do this.

_____

_____

TEKS 4.3C

20 True or false: discoveries in science are always made by scientists. Explain your answer.

_____

_____

TEKS 4.3D

21 You are asked to measure the height of a classmate. Explain what measuring tool you would use and what could be the possible result.

_____

_____

TEKS 4.2D

22 Scientists create 2-D and 3-D models of the natural world. Describe how models represent the natural world. Explain two limitations of models.

_____

_____

TEKS 4.3C

23 A student collected the following data:

1.4 cm	8 cm	3.35 cm	2.4 cm

From left to right, the measurements are numbered 1–4. Which measurement gives the most precise information?

TEKS 4.2B

Name _____ Date _____

OK

Scientific Explanations

Materials

stacks of books   2 rulers   2 marbles   plastic cup   masking tape

Procedure

A moving object will continue to move until something forces it to stop. The greater the mass of an object, the more force it takes to stop its movement. Work in groups to use empirical evidence to analyze, evaluate, and critique this scientific explanation.

❶ Prop a ruler against two books to make a ramp. Place a plastic cup at the end of the ramp with the opening facing the ramp. Use masking tape to mark the position of the cup so that you can measure the distance if it moves.

❷ Collect empirical evidence through observational testing. Roll a small marble down the ramp and into the cup. Observe and record what happens to the marble and the cup. Repeat the procedure several times and record the results.

❸ Based on the empirical evidence you have collected, use logical reasoning to form a hypothesis about what would happen if you increased the steepness of the ramp. Record your hypothesis. Use experimental testing to test your hypothesis. Add a book to the stack to increase the steepness of the ramp. Roll the small marble down the ramp and into the cup. Repeat several times, recording the results each time.

❹ Use logical reasoning and the empirical evidence you have collected to hypothesize how your results would change if you used the same three-book ramp but replaced the small marble with a large marble. Record your hypothesis. Use experimental testing to test your hypothesis. Repeat several times, recording the results each time.

❺ Analyze the empirical evidence you have collected and evaluate whether it supports the scientific explanation. Write your conclusions below.

_____

_____

_____

Scientific Explanations

Materials Performance Task sheet, stacks of books, rulers, small and large marbles, plastic cups, masking tape

Time 30 minutes

Suggested Grouping small groups

Inquiry Skills observe, use logical reasoning, hypothesize, experiment, analyze, evaluate, critique

Preparation Hints Gather sets of three books, rulers, marbles, a plastic cup, and masking tape for each group. Construct a sample model that students can follow.

Introduce the Tasks Begin the activity by discussing the scientific explanation of motion and force. Introduce the concepts with familiar examples, such as kicking and blocking a soccer ball. Help students with the concept of mass by evaluating their prior knowledge and correcting any misconceptions. Remind students of what they have learned about logical reasoning, empirical evidence, and observational and experimental testing. Tell students that they will conduct an investigation using the ruler ramp, marbles, and plastic cup to analyze, evaluate, and critique the scientific explanation.

Promote Discussion When students have finished, have the groups compare their critiques. Are they the same or different? If different, can students explain why? Were their hypotheses correct? Discuss the importance of examining all sides of scientific explanations.

Scoring Rubric

Performance Indicators

_____ Constructs and uses the ramps correctly.

_____ Uses logical reasoning to form testable hypotheses.

_____ Uses observational and experimental testing to gather and record empirical evidence.

_____ Analyzes and evaluates all sides of the scientific evidence in order to critique the scientific explanation.

Observations and Rubric Score

3   2   1   0

What Is an Engineering Design Process?

❶ Two designers believe that flatbottom boats are easier to pull on shore than other designs. How could they use observational testing to analyze and evaluate the benefits of different boat designs?

(A) brainstorm different boat designs

(B) build a model of a flatbottom boat

(C) ask people to identify the needs a boat should meet

(D) observe people pulling different boat designs on shore

❷ Janelle explains that wing design is the key to good paper airplane design. How could she use observational testing to evaluate her claim?

(A) keep records of all of her test flights

(B) test fly planes with different wing designs

(C) determine how many wing designs there are

(D) use different weights of paper to make planes

❸ What is the most important reason why researchers keep written records of their results when testing a new design?

(A) to communicate their design data

(B) to propose solutions to problems

(C) to prove that they made the design

(D) to prevent others from copying the design

❹ A camera company has just built a prototype for a new camera. The engineer explains that the new technology will prevent the camera from taking blurry pictures. What should the company do next?

(A) run experimental testing

(B) begin producing the cameras

(C) use observational testing to evaluate the engineer's claim

(D) determine what features it wants the new camera to have

❺ An engineer explains that using a lighter and stronger material will improve a company's existing sled by making a sled that is faster and easier to stop. The company is going to evaluate and critique the engineer's explanation by racing a prototype of the new sled against the company's existing sled. This is an example of which of the following?

(A) problem solving

(B) logical reasoning

(C) experimental testing

(D) observational testing

How Can You Design a Solution to a Problem?

1 Timothy designs a foam-ball wrapper for an egg. He explains that the foam protects the egg from breaking. He wants to use empirical evidence to evaluate whether his explanation is correct. What should he do?

(A) experiment with different thicknesses of foam

(B) brainstorm different ways to protect the egg from breaking

(C) drop the foam-wrapped egg from 2 meters to see if it breaks

(D) write a descriptive summary of his explanation for others to evaluate

2 An engineer explains that a different combination of engine parts will create a faster engine. How could a mechanic use experimental testing to evaluate and critique the engineer's claim?

(A) observe racecars at a racetrack

(B) test different combinations of parts

(C) read the engineer's written report

(D) create drawings of different engines

3 What would be the best way to report data on people's reactions to a new tennis shoe design?

(A) numerals

(B) concept webs

(C) labeled drawings

(D) descriptive words

4 Two students believe they have the solution to the problem of a parachute falling too quickly when it is released from a toy rocket. They explain their solution, test their design, and collect data. What should they do next?

(A) retest the model

(B) construct a model parachute

(C) analyze the results to prepare for design revisions

(D) share the test results with a company that manufactures parachutes

5 Four members of the track team test two types of shoes worn for the long jump. They want to critique a designer's claim that a new shoe design will result in longer jumps. Each jumper has a friend measure the length of the jump for each type of shoe. How should they organize their data?

(A) construct a simple table

(B) create several concept webs

(C) draw labeled pictures of the results

(D) use words to describe how the jumpers landed

What Is Technology?

❶ What inference can you make about the service claimed in this high-speed train advertisement?

> ***There Before You Know It*** trains have a 98% on-time rate! Buy your ticket today. Discounts apply to seniors. Children under 3 ride FREE!

(A) Older people ride for half price.

(B) Tickets can only be purchased today.

(C) You will arrive at your destination on schedule.

(D) High-speed trains are an example of advanced technology.

❷ Seat belts are an important part of today's automobile designs. The label on a seat belt claims that the seat belt exceeds government standards. What inference can you make about the product's claim?

(A) A second seat belt should be worn.

(B) Seat belts come in several colors.

(C) Everyone should wear a seat belt.

(D) This seat belt will keep you safe.

❸ An advertisement claims that 80% of all dogs who eat Chewy Yums dog food will grow three inches in two months. What should you do before purchasing Chewy Yums dog food?

(A) ask the store clerk about the claim

(B) evaluate the accuracy of the claim

(C) check to see if dogs like the food

(D) look at the food to see its texture

❹ A label found on the glasses shown below in this advertisement claims that people using the glasses can see songbirds for a distance of up to ten football fields away.

Why is it important to evaluate the accuracy of product claims made on labels?

(A) to make sure the product is available online

(B) to make sure the product can be purchased

(C) to make sure you are getting what you pay for

(D) to make sure the product's technology is up to date

❺ Why is it important to evaluate the accuracy of service claims found in advertisements?

(A) to check that the claim is true

(B) to make sure the service is nearby

(C) to confirm the advertisement is new

(D) to compare products being advertised

Name _____ Date _____

How Do We Use Technology?

1 Rami is building a wooden bookcase. The area for the bookcase is small, so the fit for each shelf must be correct. One of his tools is a meterstick. What design goal could this tool help him measure?

(A) wood weight

(B) wood type and color

(C) shelf length and width

(D) shelf strength and durability

2 Athena has designed a doghouse and must build a prototype. She needs to find a way to hold the pieces of wood together. She observes the design of another doghouse that has lasted a long time and carefully records the information in her notebook. What inference has she made?

(A) The design is worth copying.

(B) The doghouse has a unique design.

(C) The doghouse should be painted red.

(D) Doghouses are built in similar ways.

3 A new design for a roller coaster protects the coaster by stopping it against a large spring. To evaluate the safety of this solution, researchers build a model coaster and run it along the track. What should the researchers do?

(A) test it once to make sure it works

(B) alter the design of the roller coaster

(C) ask for suggestions concerning safety

(D) perform repeated tests to increase the reliability of the results

4 Students have designed a ride for the school fair. The ride is a cart that is pulled by ponies. The cart must travel at least 75 meters. The students separately test four design possibilities. The table below shows the test results for each change.

Change	Stopping Distance (m)
Put larger wheels on the cart	79
Use a rough wheel surface	23
Have more weight in the cart	45
Use wheels that are wider	59

What solution should the students choose for the cart?

(A) larger wheels

(B) wider wheels

(C) rough wheel surface

(D) more weight in the cart

5 A designer wants to know which type of surface works best for moving a heavy box across the ground. He sets up three different types of surfaces and measures how far the box can be pushed. He records the data and adds some notes. How should he present his information?

(A) in liters and using a table

(B) in meters and using a circle graph

(C) in numerals and using a bar graph

(D) in Celsius and using a spring scale

The Engineering Process

TEKS DOK Skill Builder

Use the following practice questions to help students build their comprehension skills for one TEKS at increasing depths of knowledge. The teacher notes below provide answers and strategies for diagnosing incorrect responses.

4.3B

Level 1: Recall and Reproduction

1. D; An advertisement provides information designed to get a message to a viewer or listener in order to sell a product or service. **Diagnose:** Students who miss this question may have confused the definitions of *advertisement* and *label*. They may also have failed to eliminate answers B and C. If students chose B or C, remind them that advertisements try to sell products and services. If students chose A, have them review the definitions of *advertisement* and *label* in the Student Edition or digital lesson.

Level 2: Skills and Concepts

2. C; It is not possible to know who the "in people" are, thus the company cannot know how many "in people" wear the shirts. **Diagnose:** Ask students to list aloud the claims the advertisement makes. Students who miss this question may have failed to consider what the claims are implying. Talk about why choices A and B are not accurate. Then help students understand that "in people" is a vague concept that cannot be measured. Thus it is not possible for the company to actually know that 9 out of 10 "in people" wear the shirts.

Level 3: Strategic Thinking

3. D; The bottom product is more nutritious because it is lower in calories, sodium, and sugars and higher in protein and vitamin C. **Diagnose:** Ask students to compare the labels. Students who miss this question may not understand the nutritional significance of the calories and the amounts of the different ingredients. Help students understand that the question calls for them to go beyond simply comparing the ingredients. They must also evaluate which amounts are better. This means that they must use their knowledge of nutrition to correctly answer the question.

The Engineering Process

Choose the letter of the best answer.

TEKS 4.3A

❶ Which term describes information designed to get across a message to a viewer or listener in order to sell something?

Ⓐ label

Ⓑ service

Ⓒ product

Ⓓ advertisement

❷ Evaluate the advertisement below.

Can you afford to let your kids be different? Everyone's wearing the famous Zedoz Hyena shirts. In Europe, Australia, New Zealand, Japan, North America, and South America, 9 out of 10 of the "in people" proudly display hyenas over their hearts.

Which statement is true about the accuracy of the claims?

Ⓐ The right clothes make a person popular.

Ⓑ Parents have a duty to make sure their children are not different.

Ⓒ It is impossible to prove that 9 out of 10 "in people" wear the shirts.

Ⓓ The company has proof that almost all of the "in people" in the world wear the shirts.

❸ Compare the food labels. What can you infer about the nutritional value of the products?

Nutrition Facts

Serving Size		Servings 4
1 container (113 g)		Calories 80
		Calories from Fat 0

Amount/Serving		%DV*
Total Fat	0g	**0%**
Trans Fat	0g	0%
Sodium	0mg	**0%**
Potassium	70mg	**2%**
Total Carb.	19g	**6%**
Dietary Fiber	<1g	3%
Sugars	18g	
Protein	0g	
Vitamin A		6%
Vitamin C		40%

*Percent Daily Values (DV) are based on a 2,000 calorie diet.
INGREDIENTS: PEACHES, WATER, SUGAR, NATURAL FLAVORS, ASCORBIC ACID (VITAMIN C), AND CITRIC ACID

Nutrition Facts

Serving Size		Servings Per Package 4
1 cup (113 g)		Calories 70
		Fat Cal. 0

Amount/Serving		%DV*
Total Fat	0g	**0%**
Saturated Fat	0g	0%
Trans Fat	0g	0%
Cholesterol	0mg	**0%**
Sodium	10mg	**0%**
Total Carb.	17g	**6%**
Dietary Fiber	<1g	2%
Sugars	16g	
Protein	<1g	
Vitamin A	4%	
Vitamin C	100%	

*Percent Daily Values (DV) are based on a 2,000 calorie diet.
INGREDIENTS: PEACHES, WATER, SUGAR, NATURAL FLAVOR, ASCORBIC ACID (TO PROTECT COLOR), CITRIC ACID

Ⓐ Neither product is nutritious.

Ⓑ Both products are equally nutritious.

Ⓒ The top product is more nutritious.

Ⓓ The bottom product is more nutritious.

The Engineering Process

Vocabulary and Concepts

1 Engineers must build a model of a design to find out how well it actually works. What is something else that engineers should do?

Ⓐ perform repeated tests to make sure the results are reliable

Ⓑ build several exact models of the design for fun

Ⓒ report what they think will be the results

Ⓓ brainstorm what the results of the test mean

TEKS 4.2E

2 Refrigerators, pencil sharpeners, and backpacks are just a few items that engineers design. Each item is required to have a label that gives information about the product. Why is it important to evaluate the information found on the label?

Ⓐ to see where the item is sold

Ⓑ to determine the energy savings

Ⓒ to know the quality of the product

Ⓓ to get the discount price for the item

TEKS 4.3B

3 People buy a service when they purchase a cell phone. What should you evaluate in advertisements for cell phones?

Ⓐ accuracy of service information

Ⓑ number of people with cell phones

Ⓒ weight and height of the cell phone

Ⓓ length of time the battery will remain charged

TEKS 4.3B

4 Metersticks and thermometers are used to collect data. How are the data gathered using these tools recorded?

Ⓐ using photos

Ⓑ using numerals

Ⓒ using drawings

Ⓓ using descriptive words

TEKS 4.2B

5 Sofia is interested in the growth of different bean seedlings. She explains that all the bean seeds sprout at similar rates. How can the other students use observational testing to analyze her explanation?

Ⓐ place seeds from different bean plants on a wet paper towel, seal them in a plastic bag, and record when they sprout

Ⓑ measure the height of three different bean seedlings two days after they have sprouted

Ⓒ research the types of bean seedlings available for the home gardener

Ⓓ investigate the differences among bean plants with a hand lens

TEKS 4.3A

6 A scientist wants to test different treadmill designs. He sees a positive advertisement for *Best Foot Forward* treadmills. What inference might he make?

Ⓐ *Best Foot Forward* is expensive.

Ⓑ *Best Foot Forward* is worth testing.

Ⓒ *Best Foot Forward* is out of date.

Ⓓ *Best Foot Forward* is a superior system.

TEKS 4.3B

7 The owner of the *Done Right* construction company claims in all of his advertisements that his company has a 98% satisfaction rate. What inference does the owner hope individuals will make?

Ⓐ Everyone can expect a lot of work for not much money.

Ⓑ The company will finish the job in a short amount of time.

Ⓒ His company is the one to hire for all construction needs.

Ⓓ Remodeling an old house can make it look like a new house.

TEKS 4.3B

8 A company has built a new type of spaceship for transporting astronauts to Mars. What should the company do before marketing its product?

Ⓐ collect data on spaceships from other investigations

Ⓑ market the spaceship as a sure way to get to Mars

Ⓒ design a prototype for the mission and market it

Ⓓ perform repeated tests of their product to increase the reliability of the results they get

TEKS 4.2E

9 An engineer has designed and built a prototype to improve the brake system of a car. What is the next step the engineer should take in the process?

Ⓐ test the working prototype

Ⓑ make sketches of the prototype

Ⓒ evaluate the design for revision

Ⓓ collect and analyze the test results

TEKS 4.2E

10 A homeowner is concerned because the old wooden steps outside her house are becoming loose. She begins to investigate stair designs. Once she has a design, what should she do next?

Ⓐ test a prototype

Ⓑ revise the design

Ⓒ build a prototype

Ⓓ decide what equipment she needs

TEKS 4.2A

11 A company decides to design and produce a new type of ice skate. It believes the skate cuts the ice better, allowing for faster skating times. It builds a prototype of the skate. What should it do next?

Ⓐ advertise the new skates

Ⓑ revise the new design and retest

Ⓒ test the new design and collect data

Ⓓ identify a need for new skates and test them

TEKS 4.2D

12 A company plans to make a new type of snow sled. The company makes several changes to its design and then measures how fast each of four designs slides down a snowy hill. It collects data on the average speeds of each design. The table below organizes the data.

Design	Change	Speed (m/s)
1	wider	2.8
2	lighter	3.2
3	longer	2.6
4	flatter	3.0

Based on the results, which design should the company use to build a faster sled?

Ⓐ 1

Ⓑ 2

Ⓒ 3

Ⓓ 4

TEKS 4.2C

13 A student is designing a new model airplane. The table shows the student's data when testing the designs. What is another way to organize this data?

Design	Speed (m/s)
1	2.9
2	2.6
3	2.9
4	2.5

Ⓐ using a bar graph

Ⓑ using a circle chart

Ⓒ using a timeline

Ⓓ using a line graph

TEKS 4.2C

14 Tabitha drops a carton of eggs while helping her father unload groceries. She believes the carton tears too easily and makes a new type of carton that would better protect the eggs.

What should Tabitha do next?

Ⓐ communicate her design plans to her teacher and classmates

Ⓑ record the steps that led up to dropping the eggs

Ⓒ collect data on her egg carton design and analyze the results

Ⓓ complain to the grocery store about the quality of the egg carton

TEKS 4.3A

15 Michael is designing a new game. As part of the planning, he needs to find out the difference in weight between a rubber ball and a foam ball. What tool should he use?

Ⓐ barometer

Ⓑ spring scale

Ⓒ pan balance

Ⓓ Celsius thermometer

TEKS 4.4A

16 Two students designed two different toy cars. They made one prototype red and the other blue. The red car moved faster but the blue one traveled farther. They carefully recorded their measurements. What should the students do next?

Ⓐ change the type of test and test again

Ⓑ analyze the data and explain the results

Ⓒ place the cars to the side and build new prototypes

Ⓓ change the colors of the cars and retest them

TEKS 4.2D

17 Diego wants to design and build a structure that will protect tomato plants from the heavy rain while still letting in sunlight. He builds four prototypes and tests each one. How should he record his data?

Ⓐ with a calculator

Ⓑ with a thermometer

Ⓒ using the metric system

Ⓓ using descriptive words

TEKS 4.2B

18 Students in a class are designing a model amusement park ride. A cart slides along a rail from the start to the finish of the ride. The students believe a smooth surface will result in the fastest speed for the cart. Which of the following would allow the students to use empirical evidence to test their claim?

Ⓐ making a design plan

Ⓑ reading a report about amusement park rides

Ⓒ testing several types of rail surfaces and recording the data

Ⓓ making labeled drawings showing different styles of rails

TEKS 4.3A

Name _____   Date _____

Apply Inquiry and Review the Big Ideas
Write the answers to these questions.

19 An engineering team is designing and producing a new type of roller coaster. Identify what they should do when testing their prototype.

_____

_____

TEKS 4.2D, 4.2E

Maxim and Laura want to design a sled. They brainstorm what shape of sled would work best on the hill in their neighborhood. Identify how they can test their ideas.

_____

TEKS 4.2B

21 A group of engineering students wants to determine how to reduce the number of accidents on a town road. The students decide to study the number of cars traveling on the road each day. Identify how the data can be measured, organized, and recorded.

_____

_____

TEKS 4.2A, 4.2D

22 A group of students is designing a new type of water bottle for a science fair project. The students know that water bottles are easily dropped during movement. Explain the problem the students must solve and describe how a solution can be tested.

_____

_____

TEKS 4.2D

23 Students test the speed of four toy car prototypes by seeing how far each travels in the same amount of time. What data should be added to the table for Prototype 2?

Prototype	Distance (cm)	Rank (fastest to slowest)
1	7	
2	3	?
3	8	1
4	4	

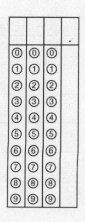

TEKS 4.2C

Evaluate Claims

Materials

Excitement and fun at home!
Enjoy hundreds of games!
Sports! Space monsters! Mazes!
Only $48.27.
Strong, well-made controls.
On-screen directions. Easy to operate.
One-year guarantee. Your money back
if not satisfied.

Nutrition Facts

Serv. size 2 oz
(56g/ box)
Servings per container 8

Calories 210
Fat Cal. 10

*Percent Daily Values (DV) are
based on a 2,000 Calorie diet.

Amount/serving	%DV*	Amount/serving
Total fat 1g	1%	Total carb. 4
Saturated fat 0g	0%	Dietary fiber 2g
Trans fat 0g		Sugars 3g
Cholesterol 0mg	0%	Protein 6g
Sodium 0mg	0%	

Vitamin A 0% • Vitamin C 0% • Calcium 2% • Iron 10%
Thiamin 30% • Riboflavin 10% • Niacin 15%

advertisements   labels

Procedure

❶ Work in small groups to examine the services and product claims found in advertisements and labels. Each group will be assigned an advertisement or label for a toy, food product, or sunscreen.

❷ Examine your assigned advertisement or label. What inferences can you draw about the services and product from the advertisement or label?

_____

_____

_____

❸ Use the table below to record the services and product claims found in your advertisement or label. Discuss the claims and evaluate their accuracy. If necessary, use the Internet to help you evaluate the claims. Record your evaluations in the table.

Product:

Claim	Evaluation

Evaluate Claims

Materials Performance Task sheet, advertisements, labels

Time 30–45 minutes

Suggested Grouping small groups

Inquiry Skills infer, evaluate, research

Preparation Hints Gather enough toy, food, and sunscreen advertisements and labels so that each group has an advertisement or label to examine and evaluate.

Introduce the Task Begin the activity by showing students examples of advertisements and product labels. Explain that in this task, groups will examine toy, food, and sunscreen advertisements and labels in order to draw inferences about the services and products and evaluate the accuracy of the claims. Use a sample advertisement to model the performance task. Work as a class to draw an inference. Then identify the claims being made in the advertisement. Encourage students to use the Internet to gather information to help them evaluate the accuracy of their group's advertisement or label.

Promote Discussion Have groups share their inferences and evaluations. Ask volunteers to tell how they drew their inferences and the processes they used to evaluate the claims. Discuss the importance of evaluating the claims made in advertisements and labels.

Scoring Rubric

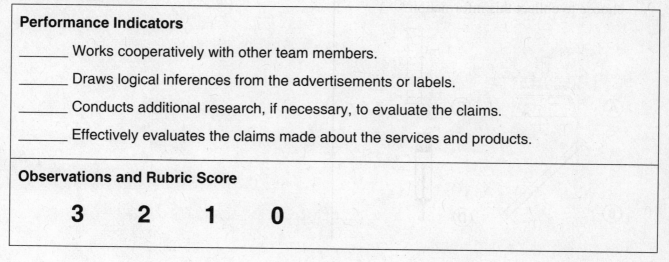

Performance Indicators

_____ Works cooperatively with other team members.

_____ Draws logical inferences from the advertisements or labels.

_____ Conducts additional research, if necessary, to evaluate the claims.

_____ Effectively evaluates the claims made about the services and products.

Observations and Rubric Score

3   2   1   0

What Are Physical Properties of Matter?

1 Miguel is thinking of all of the ways he can contrast the size of two objects. He has thought of measuring each object's weight and volume. What is one tool he could use to measure another difference in size?

Ⓐ computer
Ⓑ metric ruler
Ⓒ collecting net
Ⓓ thermometer

2 You can use tools to compare properties of matter. What property would you be comparing if you collected measurements using a Celsius thermometer?

Ⓐ mass
Ⓑ weight
Ⓒ volume
Ⓓ temperature

3 Barack wants to measure the volume of a marble. Which instrument should he choose to collect this information?

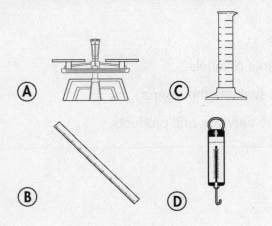

4 Lara uses a balance to measure the mass of some snap-together blocks. The mass of a red block is 3 g, of a blue block is 5 g, and of a yellow block is 7 g. She then makes a toy building using three of each type of block. If she measures the mass of the building, what would it most likely be?

Ⓐ 44 g
Ⓑ 45 g
Ⓒ 46 g
Ⓓ 49 g

5 James observes a tennis ball and a basketball on the table. Which property of matter can he compare without any measurement tools?

Ⓐ size
Ⓑ weight
Ⓒ volume
Ⓓ density

What Objects Will Sink or Float?

1 The ability to float is one property of matter. Compare the following objects. Which one can float in water?

(A) a cork

(B) a key

(C) a brick

(D) a marble

2 Deborah sets up a test to contrast the ability of a foam ball, a tennis ball, a baseball, a basketball, and a beach ball to sink or float. She would like to make a chart to organize the data she collects. How should she organize her data?

(A) by size of ball

(B) by type of ball

(C) by the ability to sink or float

(D) by the material each ball is made of

3 Malik places a small cube of wood into a beaker filled with water. The wood floats on top of the water. Which of these best explains why the wood block floats?

(A) Most objects will float on water.

(B) The wood cube is less dense than the water.

(C) The wood cube has less mass than the water.

(D) The water has more volume than the wood cube.

4 A scientist uses a graduated cylinder filled with water to compare physical properties of a marble, a small rock, and a wooden stick. Which two physical properties is he measuring?

(A) mass and weight

(B) length and volume

(C) volume and the ability to float

(D) weight and the ability to float

5 Kellie constructs the chart below from observations written in her Science Notebook.

Floats	Sinks
tennis ball	
	eraser
beach ball	
	paper clip
	screw

Compare and contrast the data. What is one conclusion that you should draw from this chart?

(A) All balls float.

(B) All small objects float.

(C) All larger objects sink.

(D) Size is not the reason an object sinks or floats.

What Are the States of Water?

❶ Compare the states of matter. What happens when water changes from a gas to a liquid?

(A) It melts.

(B) It freezes.

(C) It evaporates.

(D) It condenses.

❷ Joseph collected a handful of hail and placed it in the freezer. If Joseph were to compare the hail he collected with ice cubes kept in the freezer, what would he conclude?

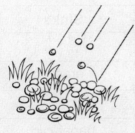

(A) They are the same state of matter.

(B) They are different states of matter.

(C) They change states at different temperatures.

(D) The hail will change state when placed in the freezer.

❸ Contrast physical properties of matter. What happens as liquid water becomes ice?

(A) It does not change states.

(B) It changes from a liquid to a solid.

(C) It changes from a solid to a gas.

(D) It changes from a gas to a solid.

❹ On a hot summer day, Jenna poured juice into an ice cube tray. She put the tray into the freezer. When she removed the tray, the juice was frozen. She measured, or counted, the states of matter. Which number tells how many changes of state took place from the time Jenna poured the juice until she took it out of the freezer?

(A) 1

(B) 2

(C) 3

(D) 4

❺ You can contrast the properties of water. You can take ice cubes from a freezer and put them in a glass. You can put water from a faucet into a pot and boil it on the stove. Where will you find water as a liquid turning into a gas?

(A) in the glass

(B) in the freezer

(C) on the stove

(D) from the faucet

How Does Water Change States?

❶ Three states of matter are solid, liquid, and gas. During which process does water vapor become liquid water?

- Ⓐ melting
- Ⓑ freezing
- Ⓒ evaporation
- Ⓓ condensation

❷ A student has a pot full of water. He wants to contrast physical properties of matter. How can he use energy to cause the liquid water to become water vapor?

- Ⓐ add heat by placing the pot on a hot plate
- Ⓑ add ice cubes to the water and place it outside
- Ⓒ stir the water several times and place it in the refrigerator
- Ⓓ place the pot of water in the freezer and leave it for three hours

❸ Water changes states when energy is added or taken away. Suppose you collect data by measuring, and you find that the outside air temperature has fallen from 10 °C to below 0 °C. If you place liquid water outside, how do you predict it will change as it cools?

- Ⓐ It will melt into a solid.
- Ⓑ It will freeze into a solid.
- Ⓒ It will evaporate into a vapor.
- Ⓓ It will condense into a liquid.

❹ A scientist is interested in the mass of water and ice. He collects data on the mass of ice placed in a beaker. He then melts the ice in the beaker and collects data on the mass of the liquid water in the beaker. He subtracts the mass of the beaker from each measurement. Which tool does he use to collect data on the mass of matter?

- Ⓐ a barometer
- Ⓑ a spring scale
- Ⓒ a thermometer
- Ⓓ a triple beam balance

❺ All matter is made of particles. Contrast the physical properties of matter. How are particles arranged in different states of matter?

- Ⓐ The particles in gases are farther apart than the particles in solids.
- Ⓑ The particles in gases are closer together than the particles in solids.
- Ⓒ The particles in most solids are farther apart than the particles in liquids.
- Ⓓ The particles in most gases are closer together than the particles in liquids.

What Are Some Physical Changes?

1 Ren takes a stick of butter from the refrigerator and leaves it on the table in a room that is very warm. Which is a physical change you predict will occur to the butter as a result of heating?

Ⓐ Its taste will change.

Ⓑ Its shape will change.

Ⓒ It will gain new ingredients.

Ⓓ It will become a different substance.

2 Compare and contrast the variety of solutions and mixtures given in the chart.

Beaker 1	water and sand
Beaker 2	water and lemon juice
Beaker 3	water and marbles
Beaker 4	water and salt

Which beaker contains a solution formed by dissolving a solid in a liquid?

Ⓐ Beaker 1

Ⓑ Beaker 2

Ⓒ Beaker 3

Ⓓ Beaker 4

3 Which would you construct to evaluate data on three tests showing how long it takes for three different solutions to form?

Ⓐ a timeline

Ⓑ a circle graph

Ⓒ a bar graph

Ⓓ a set of photos

4 Kyle planned to take ice cubes from the freezer and set them out on the counter.

What did he most likely predict would immediately occur?

Ⓐ Heat would move from the air to the ice.

Ⓑ Heat would move from the ice to the air.

Ⓒ Heat would cause the liquid water to freeze.

Ⓓ Heat would move between the two ice cubes.

5 Ji-hun is oiling the wheels of his skateboard. He tries to wash the oil off his hands with only water, but nothing happens. What would happen if he added a few drops of dish soap?

Ⓐ The oil would stick to his hands.

Ⓑ The oil would change into a gas.

Ⓒ The oil, water, and soap would form a solution.

Ⓓ The soap would help break up the oil into smaller drops.

How Can We Make a Solution?

❶ For which observation would you record data using descriptive words instead of numerical data?

- Ⓐ the appearance of three different solutions
- Ⓑ the time it takes for a substance to dissolve in a second substance
- Ⓒ a comparison of the volumes of three solutions
- Ⓓ a comparison of the mass of three solutions

❷ Water, drink mix, and sugar are mixed in a pitcher. Hot water, instant coffee, sugar, and cream are mixed in a coffee cup. Compare and contrast these solutions. Which substance is the solvent in one or both?

- Ⓐ cream
- Ⓑ water
- Ⓒ sugar
- Ⓓ coffee

❸ A student observes the condition of three backyard ponds and constructs a chart to organize her data. She states that Pond A is muddy, Pond B has lily pads floating on clear water, and Pond C is dried up. In constructing a reasonable explanation, she determines that—

- Ⓐ the water in Pond B is a solution
- Ⓑ the water in Pond C was a mixture
- Ⓒ the water in Pond A is a solution
- Ⓓ the water in Pond B is a mixture

❹ Martina's science class is learning about mixtures and solutions. Her teacher shows the class four beakers.

Which beaker contains a solution?

- Ⓐ Beaker A
- Ⓑ Beaker B
- Ⓒ Beaker C
- Ⓓ Beaker D

❺ Shontal is observing how quickly a tablespoon of salt dissolves in water. She is wondering if other substances dissolve as easily. Which of the following could she use for comparison?

- Ⓐ sugar mixed into water
- Ⓑ pepper mixed into water
- Ⓒ birdseed mixed into water
- Ⓓ tea leaves mixed into water

Matter

TEKS DOK Skill Builder

Use the following practice questions to help students build their comprehension skills for one TEKS at increasing depths of knowledge. The teacher notes below provide answers and strategies for diagnosing incorrect responses.

4.5A

Level 1: Recall and Reproduction

1. D; The volume is 64 cubic centimeters. The volume of a solid block is calculated by multiplying the width by the length by the height. **Diagnose:** Students who miss this question did not remember the formula. If students chose A, they added the numbers. If students chose B, they multiplied only two of the numbers. If students chose C, they added two numbers and then multiplied by the remaining number. Have students who missed this question review the formula for finding the volume of a solid rectangle in the Student Edition or digital lesson.

Level 2: Skills and Concepts

2. A; Both blocks have the same volume. To get the correct answer, students must find the volume of both blocks and then compare the volumes. **Diagnose:** Ask students who miss this question to explain the process they used to find the answer. Students who chose B may have guessed based on a comparison of size. Students who chose C or D used the wrong formula before comparing the volumes. Have students who missed this question review the formula for finding the volume of a solid rectangle in the Student Edition or digital lesson.

Level 3: Strategic Thinking

3. C; The jar of popped popcorn floats because the particles in the popcorn are farther apart than the particles in the water. **Diagnose:** Ask students why some objects float and others sink. If students say some objects float because they are less dense, ask what makes one object less dense than another. Students who miss this question are not making the connection between density and how close together the particles in an object are. They may also be confusing which arrangement of particles makes an object more or less dense. Have students who missed this question review the discussion of density and the arrangement of particles in the Student Edition or digital lesson.

Matter

Choose the letter of the best answer.

`TEKS` **4.5A**

❶ Find the volume of the solid block below.

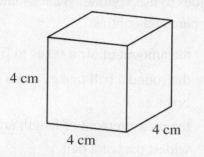

4 cm

4 cm   4 cm

- Ⓐ 12 cubic centimeters
- Ⓑ 16 cubic centimeters
- Ⓒ 32 cubic centimeters
- Ⓓ 64 cubic centimeters

❷ Ana measured two blocks so that she could compare their volumes.

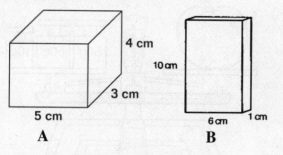

4 cm

10 cm

3 cm

5 cm   6 cm   1 cm

A   **B**

Which statement describes what she found?

- Ⓐ The volumes are the same.
- Ⓑ Block B has a smaller volume than block A.
- Ⓒ The volume of block B is 5 cm greater than block A.
- Ⓓ The volume of block A is 16 cm greater than block B.

❸ Marcus plans an experiment on density. He fills one small glass jar with popped popcorn and another small glass jar with marbles. He places both jars in a beaker of water. The jar of popped popcorn floats. The jar of marbles sinks. What conclusion does Marcus draw from his experiment?

- Ⓐ The particles in the marbles are farther apart than the particles in the water, so the marbles are more dense than the water.
- Ⓑ The particles in the marbles are closer together than the particles in the water, so the marbles are less dense than the water.
- Ⓒ The particles in the popped popcorn are farther apart than the particles in the water, so the popcorn is less dense than the water.
- Ⓓ The particles in the popped popcorn are closer together than the particles in the water, so the popcorn is less dense than the water.

Matter

Vocabulary and Concepts

1 Genelle enjoys working with mixtures and solutions. With which science career might she connect?

(A) chemist

(B) physicist

(C) meteorologist

(D) environmentalist

TEKS 4.3D

2 An artist is creating a piece of art using fabric. It will be placed inside a box. Individuals will place their hands in the box, touch the art without being able to see it, and describe a physical property of the art. The descriptions will be recorded in a notebook. How are data being collected?

(A) using measurements

(B) using descriptive words

(C) using images of the touched art

(D) using drawings of what was felt

TEKS 4.2B

3 Marcus makes salad dressing. He puts 150 mL of oil and 150 mL of vinegar in a jar and shakes it. After 5 minutes, the oil is on top of the vinegar. What can Marcus conclude about the salad dressing?

(A) More vinegar is needed to dissolve the oil.

(B) More oil is needed to dissolve the vinegar.

(C) The oil and vinegar have formed a mixture.

(D) The oil and vinegar have formed a solution.

TEKS 4.5C

4 Karen wants to use a physical property to compare and contrast three balls. She decides to use volume. What should she compare and contrast?

(A) the amount of air it takes to fill a ball

(B) the sound a ball makes when it bounces

(C) the measurement of length around the widest part of a ball

(D) the measurement of length from one side of a ball to the other

TEKS 4.5A

5 Aaron uses the pan balance below to measure the mass of the apple. What does Aaron learn?

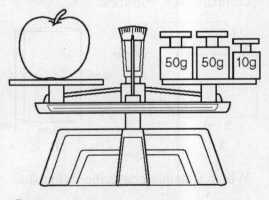

(A) The apple's mass is 10 g.

(B) The apple's mass is 50 g.

(C) The apple's mass is 101 g.

(D) The apple's mass is 110 g.

TEKS 4.5A

6 An inventor wants to build a surfboard that is the best one on the market. Which physical property of the material used to make the surfboard will she need to measure?

- (A) its ability to insulate
- (B) its ability to sink or float
- (C) its ability to conduct electricity
- (D) its ability to be attracted by magnets

TEKS 4.5A

7 Water changes states when energy is added or taken away. Predict what will happen to liquid water when heat is added.

- (A) It will melt into a gas.
- (B) It will evaporate as water vapor.
- (C) It will freeze and become ice.
- (D) It will condense into water droplets.

TEKS 4.5B

8 In which test below would a spring scale be used?

- (A) when collecting information on the mass of a chunk of volcanic rock
- (B) when collecting information on the weight of a box that will be pushed
- (C) when collecting information on the volume of a solution in a beaker
- (D) when collecting information on the speed of a toy car going downhill

TEKS 4.4A

9 The simple chart below was constructed to compare some properties of water in different states.

Solid	Liquid	Gas
has a definite shape	?	expands to fill its container

Which property should be put into the second column?

- (A) tastes stale
- (B) feels smooth
- (C) has a strong odor
- (D) takes the shape of its container

TEKS 4.2C, 4.5A

10 Water is found as a liquid, a solid, and a gas. Predict how liquid water will change if it is cooled suddenly.

- (A) Ice will quickly form.
- (B) Evaporation will occur.
- (C) Condensation will occur.
- (D) Little change will result.

TEKS 4.5B

11 Daniel designs a toy boat. He chooses five different materials and sets up an investigation to compare their physical properties. What physical property will the material for his boat need to have?

- (A) be highly reflective
- (B) be able to float
- (C) be denser than water
- (D) be a good conductor of heat

TEKS 4.5A

12 Javier makes three balls out of clay. He puts all the clay balls on a balance and measures the total mass as 56 g. He then molds the clay into one big ball and measures its mass, which is 56 g. Analyze Javier's data to construct a reasonable explanation for his findings.

(A) He measured incorrectly and should measure again.

(B) The whole is equal to the sum of its parts.

(C) The clay gains mass when it is one large ball.

(D) Dividing the clay resulted in some of it being lost.

TEKS 4.2D, 4.5A

13 Deb measures the mass of four rock samples. She constructs the bar graph below to organize her data.

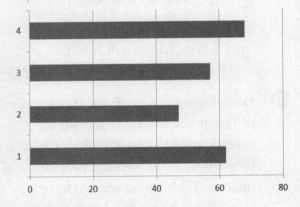

How should the data be labeled along the horizontal axis?

(A) Liters (L)

(B) Samples

(C) Grams (g)

(D) Results

TEKS 4.2B, 4.2C

14 Biodegradable materials break down quickly in the environment. People make informed choices in the recycling of materials based on the physical properties of matter. Which of the following materials has the physical properties that allow it to quickly biodegrade?

(A) rubber ball

(B) banana peel

(C) plastic bottle

(D) aluminum can

TEKS 4.1B

15 Compare mixtures that you can identify. What do all of the mixtures have in common?

(A) They are a combination of substances that give off a gas.

(B) They are any type of matter that can change its shape or color.

(C) They are any type of matter that evaporates when heat is added.

(D) They are a combination of two or more substances that keep their identities.

TEKS 4.5C

16 Solutions come in many forms. Which of the following is a solution?

(A) a gram of sugar

(B) a handful of soil

(C) a liter of salt water

(D) a cup of noodle soup

TEKS 4.5C

17 Which physical property of matter does a thermometer measure?

   Ⓐ mass

   Ⓑ density

   Ⓒ volume

   Ⓓ temperature

TEKS 4.5A

18 What is a physical property shared by iron, nickel, and steel?

   Ⓐ size

   Ⓑ magnetism

   Ⓒ ease of bending

   Ⓓ inability to rust

TEKS 4.5A

Apply Inquiry and Review the Big Ideas
Write the answers to these questions.

19 Contrast a mixture and a solution. Give one example of a mixture or one example of a solution.

_____

_____

TEKS 4.5C

20 Some of the ice in a student's tea melts. Explain why.

_____

_____

TEKS 4.5A

21 Does a change of state affect the amount of matter in a sample of water? Explain.

_____

_____

TEKS 4.5A

Name ____________________________ Date __________

22 Study the following group of items. Put the items into two groups according to their physical properties. Describe the properties you used to classify the objects.

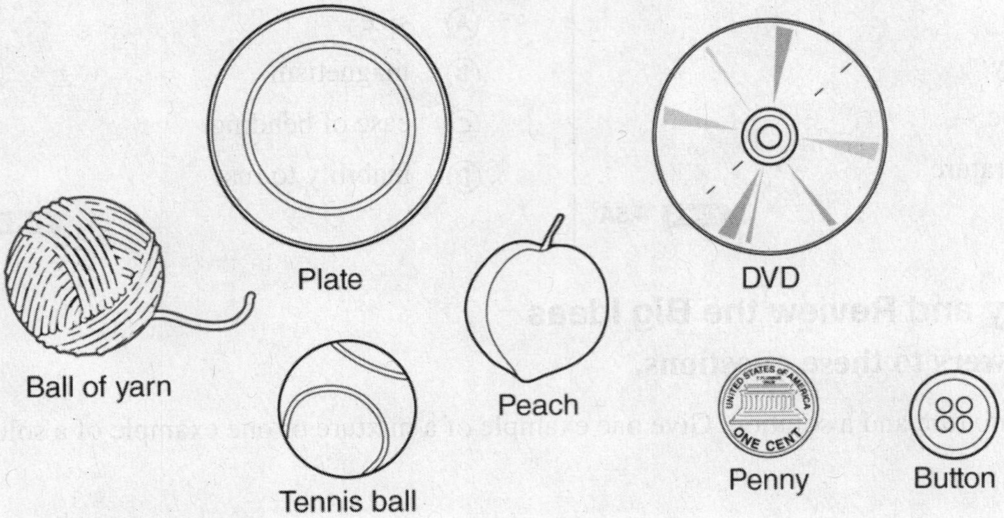
Plate
DVD
Ball of yarn
Peach
Tennis ball
Penny
Button
UNITED STATES OF AMERICA
ONE CENT

____

____

____

____

____

____

TEKS 4.5A

23 A student uses a pan balance to measure the mass of a toy truck. He records the mass in a chart. He then takes the truck apart and places all the parts on the pan balance. What will the student record in his chart below as the mass of the truck's parts?

Object	Mass
Whole truck	92 grams
Truck taken apart	? grams

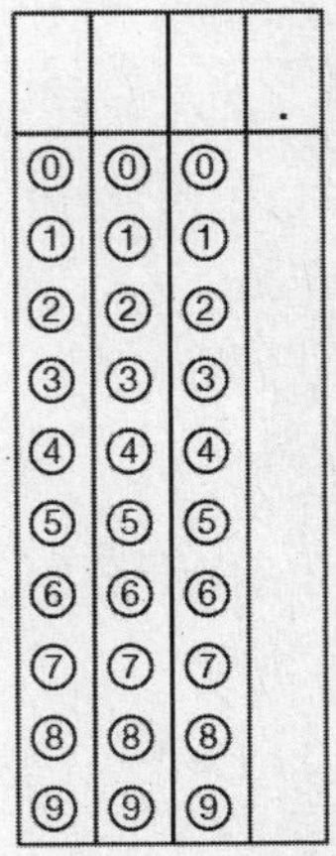

TEKS 4.5A

Student Task

Measure Matter

Materials

metric ruler   pan balance   beaker   magnet

Procedure

Work in small groups to measure, compare, and contrast the physical properties of different samples of matter. Your teacher will provide the objects to measure.

1 Use a metric ruler to measure the size of each object. Determine its length or width.

2 Use a pan balance to measure the mass of each object.

3 Use a beaker to measure the volume of each object. After measuring the volume, determine whether the object sinks or floats.

4 Use a magnet to measure whether each object has the property of magnetism. Observe how the object reacts to the magnet.

5 Record your findings in a data table like the one below. Add a row for each object you measure. Use the table to examine and evaluate your data.

Object	Size	Mass	Volume	Sink or Float	Magnetism

6 Compare and contrast the objects based on their properties of size, mass, volume, magnetism, and the ability to sink or float.

_____

_____

_____

_____

Measure Matter

Materials Performance Task sheet, small rock, steel bolt, glass marble, wood block, plastic toy, large nail, metric ruler, pan balance, beaker, magnet

Time 30–45 minutes

Suggested Grouping small groups

Inquiry Skills measure, compare, contrast, record, evaluate

Preparation Hints Gather enough materials so that each group has one of each item.

Introduce the Task Explain that in this task, students will be required to measure matter, record data, and compare and contrast physical properties of matter. Identify each tool used for measuring. If necessary, demonstrate how to measure the length, mass, and volume of one item included in the materials list. Explain that magnetism is a property of some matter. Demonstrate how to use a magnet to determine magnetism.

Promote Discussion Have students share any problems they may have had with measuring. Review proper procedures, if necessary. Hold up each object and have students share what they learned about its physical properties—including magnetism and whether it sinks or floats.

Scoring Rubric

Performance Indicators
_____ Works cooperatively with other team members.
_____ Accurately measures items.
_____ Correctly compares similar physical properties.
_____ Correctly contrasts different physical properties.

Observations and Rubric Score
3   **2**   **1**   **0**

What Are Some Forms of Energy?

❶ A light bulb converts electrical energy into which of the following?

- Ⓐ light only
- Ⓑ heat only
- Ⓒ heat and light
- Ⓓ light and motion

❷ What energy change takes place when Sam plugs a radio into an electrical outlet?

- Ⓐ Light energy changes into sound energy.
- Ⓑ Electrical energy changes into sound energy.
- Ⓒ Sound energy changes into electrical energy.
- Ⓓ Chemical energy changes into sound energy.

❸ What form of energy conversion is taking place in this steamboat?

- Ⓐ Light energy changes into sound energy.
- Ⓑ Heat energy changes into mechanical energy.
- Ⓒ Light energy changes into electrical energy.
- Ⓓ Electrical energy changes into mechanical energy.

❹ Differentiate among the forms of energy shown in the diagram below.

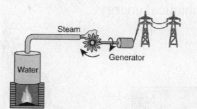

Which kind of energy conversion occurs in the generator?

- Ⓐ sound energy into electrical energy
- Ⓑ mechanical energy into electrical energy
- Ⓒ electrical energy into mechanical energy
- Ⓓ electrical energy into heat

❺ These solar panels produce energy for homes and businesses. Which kind of energy conversion occurs within these panels?

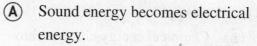

- Ⓐ Sound energy becomes electrical energy.
- Ⓑ Electrical energy becomes light energy.
- Ⓒ Mechanical energy becomes light energy.
- Ⓓ Light energy becomes electrical energy.

Name _____ Date _____

Where Does Energy Come From?

❶ Differentiate among forms of energy. Which object converts electrical energy into mechanical energy?

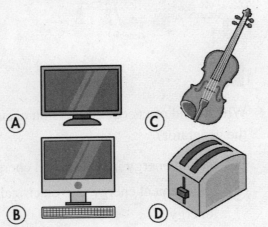

Ⓐ

Ⓑ

Ⓒ

Ⓓ

❷ What change in energy takes place when a wind turbine is used to generate energy?

Ⓐ Wind energy becomes chemical energy.

Ⓑ Sound energy becomes light energy.

Ⓒ Mechanical energy becomes electrical energy.

Ⓓ Electrical energy changes to heat.

❸ Which form of energy conversion takes place in a gas-powered lawnmower?

Ⓐ Light energy changes into sound energy.

Ⓑ Chemical energy changes into mechanical energy.

Ⓒ Light energy changes into electrical energy.

Ⓓ Sound energy changes into mechanical energy.

❹ The girl shown below is using an electrical appliance that has a motor.

Differentiate among the forms of energy. Which energy conversion is taking place?

Ⓐ electrical energy into thermal energy and mechanical energy

Ⓑ electrical energy into sound energy and chemical energy

Ⓒ sound energy into electrical energy and mechanical energy

Ⓓ mechanical energy into electrical energy

❺ Solar panels produce energy for homes and businesses. Which kind of energy conversion occurs within these panels?

Ⓐ Sound energy becomes electrical energy.

Ⓑ Light energy becomes electrical energy.

Ⓒ Mechanical energy becomes light energy.

Ⓓ Electrical energy becomes light energy.

Name _____ Date _____

How Does Heat Move?

❶ Mary uses a thermometer to take a single reading of water in a beaker. What is she measuring?

Ⓐ how fast the water warms in the beaker

Ⓑ how hot or cold the water in the beaker is

Ⓒ amount of energy transferred from the beaker to the water

Ⓓ amount of energy transferred from the water to the beaker

❷ On a warm sunny day, a lizard sits on a rock. Differentiate among the forms of energy listed below. Which term explains why the lizard feels warmth from the sun?

Ⓐ sound energy

Ⓑ electrical energy

Ⓒ thermal energy

Ⓓ mechanical energy

❸ A student learns that heat can be transferred between two objects that are in direct contact. This is conduction. Which is an example of conduction?

Ⓐ a light is turned on

Ⓑ your hand causes a snowball to melt

Ⓒ a turbine turns inside a generator

Ⓓ the sun shines into a greenhouse

❹ The chart below shows some sources of heat.

1	rays of the sun
2	electric space heater
3	oven with a fan
4	hot plate

Differentiate among the forms of energy by identifying convection in the chart.

Ⓐ row 1 only

Ⓑ rows 1 and 2

Ⓒ rows 2 and 3

Ⓓ rows 3 and 4

❺ Which picture shows the transfer of heat by both conduction and convection?

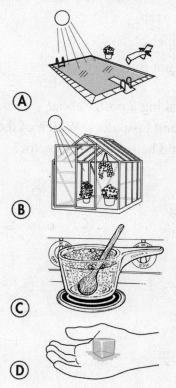

Ⓐ

Ⓑ

Ⓒ

Ⓓ

What Are Conductors and Insulators?

1 Maxwell is going to stir some soup he is cooking in a pot. The soup is very hot. He wants to use a spoon that will keep his hand from getting too hot. Differentiate between conductors and insulators in the list below. Which material should he use?

(A) aluminum

(B) copper

(C) steel

(D) wood

2 Carissa is planning to take a hot sandwich to school for lunch. She wants to wrap it in something to keep it warm. If she correctly differentiates between insulators and conductors, which wrap will she choose?

(A) foam wrap

(B) plastic wrap

(C) wax paper

(D) aluminum foil

3 Jeffrey is making a poster about conductors and insulators. Which of these objects should he list as a conductor?

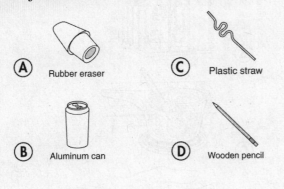

(A) Rubber eraser

(C) Plastic straw

(B) Aluminum can

(D) Wooden pencil

4 Mr. Jacobsen is watching some builders while they are putting up the walls of a house. He notices that there is a small space between the outer and inner walls of the house. Differentiate between conductors and insulators. Which of the following will the builders most likely use as an insulator between the outer and inner walls?

(A) plastic foam

(B) layers of wood

(C) shredded paper

(D) thick aluminum

5 Lenora is going outside to play on a cold winter day. Which feature of her winter coat will insulate her from the cold?

(A) It is lightweight.

(B) It has fur at the edges.

(C) It is thick and very fluffy.

(D) It has a single layer of cloth.

How Do Conductors and Insulators Differ?

1 Stephanie pours equal amounts of hot water into four cups. Each cup is made of a different material. She puts a thermometer into each cup and collects information using a stopwatch to indicate when 3 minutes have elapsed.

Foam   Metal   Paper   Plastic

She constructs a chart to organize her data. What data will she add to her chart?

(A) four types of material and different temperatures

(B) similar materials and similar temperatures

(C) similar temperatures for each type of material

(D) four types of material and three different temperatures

2 Differentiate between conductors and insulators. Which material keeps heat out of a garden shed during summer?

(A) steel

(B) wood

(C) copper

(D) aluminum

3 Deborah needs a good insulator. Which material should she choose?

(A) iron

(B) steel

(C) foam

(D) copper

4 Liam places ten cold items in a metal lunchbox and ten cold items in a foam lunchbox to see if they will stay cold. He plans to collect data on his test when he gets to school.

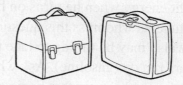

Liam constructs a chart to describe how the items feel after he arrives at school. He then analyzes the data. What does he conclude about the insulating ability of the lunchboxes?

(A) Metal is better than foam.

(B) Foam and metal are equal.

(C) Foam is better than metal.

(D) Neither kept the items cold.

5 Differentiate between conductors and insulators. Which of the following is a good conductor?

(A) wood chips

(B) plastic bags

(C) newspapers

(D) copper wire

Forms of Energy

TEKS DOK Skill Builder

Use the following practice questions to help students build their comprehension skills for one TEKS at increasing depths of knowledge. The teacher notes below provide answers and strategies for diagnosing incorrect responses.

4.6A

Level 1: Recall and Reproduction

1. C; The hot pot on the stove is an example of thermal energy. **Diagnose:** Students who miss this question may not associate thermal energy with heat. Have students who miss this question review the discussion of thermal energy and heat in the Student Edition or digital lesson.

Level 2: Skills and Concepts

2. D; The car's engine changes the chemical energy in gasoline to mechanical energy when Tim's mom presses the gas pedal to drive. The process also produces heat. Tim changes electrical energy to light energy when he turns on his desk lamp. The light bulb also gives off heat. **Diagnose:** Students who miss this question may be confused about one or more sources of energy. They also may be failing to take the order of change into consideration. Ask students what most cars run on (gasoline). Ask what kind of energy gasoline produces (chemical). Have students look for the answers that begin with chemical energy. Then ask what kind of energy a moving car has (mechanical). Have students find the answer that includes chemical energy changing into mechanical energy. Help them understand that this change sequence eliminates all but one answer. Help students see that D is the correct answer by doing the same exercise for the lamp. Have students who are still having difficulty review the Student Edition or digital lesson to strengthen their understanding of each type of energy and the ways in which energy changes form.

Level 3: Strategic Thinking

3. D; When the coins are rubbed, the particles move more quickly, producing thermal energy. The faster the particles move, the more thermal energy is produced. The thermal energy is transferred as heat. **Diagnose:** Students who miss this question are not associating rubbing with thermal energy or heat with the transfer of energy. Remind students of the Student Edition discussion of rubbing one's hands together to make them warm. Explain that the coins work in the same way. Help students associate the fast movement of particles with the production of thermal energy. Examine each answer so that students can eliminate the answers that do not focus on thermal energy, the movement of particles, and the transfer of heat. Then help students understand the order of the change. If students still have difficulty understanding why D is the correct answer, have them review the discussion of thermal energy and heat in the Student Edition or digital lesson.

Forms of Energy

Choose the letter of the best answer.

TEKS 4.6A

❶ Which picture is an example of thermal energy?

Ⓐ

Ⓑ

Ⓒ

Ⓓ

❷ Tim's mother starts the car and drives Tim home from school. When Tim gets home, he turns on his desk lamp. What changes in forms of energy have occurred?

Ⓐ car: electrical → mechanical; lamp: light → heat

Ⓑ car: chemical → electrical; lamp: electrical → light

Ⓒ car: electrical → chemical; lamp: mechanical → light

Ⓓ car: chemical → mechanical and heat; lamp: electrical → light and heat

❸ As Ellie rubs two coins together, the coins become warm. Which statement correctly explains why this happens?

Ⓐ The rubbing action changes chemical energy into mechanical energy, which is transferred as heat.

Ⓑ The rubbing action produces heat as the particles in the coins vibrate. The heat is transferred as thermal energy.

Ⓒ The rubbing action produces mechanical energy, which is transferred as heat and chemical energy.

Ⓓ The rubbing action produces thermal energy as the particles in the coins move faster. The thermal energy is transferred as heat.

Forms of Energy

Vocabulary and Concepts

❶ The pots and pans in Tyson's kitchen are made of steel, copper, and aluminum. Why does his family use metal pans for cooking?

Ⓐ They are easy to shape.

Ⓑ They have low melting points.

Ⓒ They are excellent conductors of heat.

Ⓓ They have the ability to stop the flow of heat.

TEKS 4.6B

❷ Which of these appliances is intended to convert electrical energy into sound energy?

Ⓐ printer

Ⓑ refrigerator

Ⓒ electric heater

Ⓓ music amplifier

TEKS 4.6A

❸ A physicist studies how energy and matter are related. She must know math, chemistry, and the principles of energy transfer. Connect science concepts with science careers. Which might a physicist study?

Ⓐ how plants can resist diseases

Ⓑ how a waterfall could produce electricity

Ⓒ how food webs can be affected when the environment is disturbed

Ⓓ how water cycles through the environment from groundwater to water vapor

TEKS 4.3D

❹ An insulator is often used to help regulate an object's temperature. Differentiate between insulators and conductors. Which is true about an insulator?

Ⓐ It slows energy transfer.

Ⓑ It can also be a good conductor.

Ⓒ It allows heat to pass through easily.

Ⓓ It provides heat to keep materials warm.

TEKS 4.6B

❺ The diagram below shows how the flow of water turns a turbine. Electricity is generated. Differentiate among the forms of energy shown in the diagram.

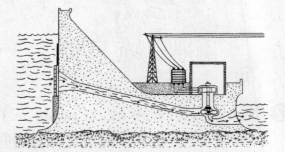

Which kind of energy conversion takes place in the turbine?

Ⓐ electrical energy into sound energy

Ⓑ energy of motion into light energy

Ⓒ thermal energy into mechanical energy

Ⓓ mechanical energy into electrical energy

TEKS 4.6A

6 Rene wears wool socks with her winter boots to keep her feet warm. Differentiate between conductors and insulators. How does the wool affect heat transfer?

(A) Wool is an insulator that keeps Rene's feet from losing heat.

(B) Wool is an insulator that provides heat to keep Rene's feet warm.

(C) Wool is a conductor that transfers heat from Rene's feet to her boots.

(D) Wool is a conductor that transfers heat from the socks to Rene's skin.

TEKS 4.6B

7 Two science students put a spring on a dowel. Then they add a foam ball to the dowel. They push on the ball to squeeze the spring, and then they let the ball go. Differentiate among the forms of energy listed below. Which form of energy does the ball have during the investigation?

(A) thermal energy

(B) electrical energy

(C) magnetic energy

(D) mechanical energy

TEKS 4.6A

8 Which type of material would be best to use to keep hot food from getting cold?

(A) wood

(B) paper

(C) rubber

(D) aluminum

TEKS 4.6B

9 Mila is studying mechanical energy. She tapes a dowel onto a desk. Then she puts a 12 cm spring on the dowel. Next, she slips a foam ball onto the dowel. As she changes the length of the spring by compressing it, she releases the ball into the air. She does this several times.

Length of compressed spring (cm)	Distance traveled by ball (m)
10	2
8	2.5
6	4
4	6

What happens to the ball as Mila changes the length of the spring?

(A) When the spring is longer, the ball travels farther.

(B) When the spring is longer, the ball does not move.

(C) When the spring is shorter, the ball travels farther.

(D) When the spring is shorter, the ball does not move.

TEKS 4.2C, 4.6A

10 The pictures below show different household items. Differentiate between conductors and insulators. Which item is a good conductor of heat?

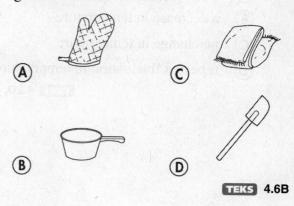

(A)

(B)

(C)

(D)

TEKS 4.6B

11 Inez enjoys learning about different forms of energy. She especially likes to study electrical energy. She wonders how to make energy use more efficient. She wants to study how technology can be used to conserve energy to reduce the use of fossil fuels. What career might Inez connect with in her future studies?

(A) biologist

(B) zoologist

(C) electrical engineer

(D) electrician

TEKS 4.3D

12 Differentiate among forms of energy. This thermometer was in the shade.

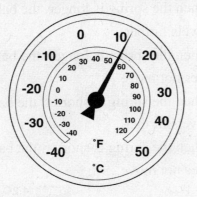

The sun began to shine on the thermometer. After 15 minutes, what will the thermometer show?

(A) an increase in temperature

(B) a decrease in temperature

(C) no change in temperature

(D) repeated fluctuation in temperature

TEKS 4.2D, 4.6A

13 Differentiate among forms of energy. Which type of energy allows people to hear the music during a middle school band concert?

(A) light

(B) sound

(C) thermal

(D) electrical

TEKS 4.6A

14 Mark places a cold pat of butter on a slice of hot toasted bread. The butter melts. Which statement below explains why the butter melts?

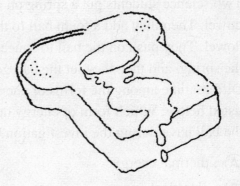

(A) The hot toast quickly cools when the butter is placed on it.

(B) Heat moves from a cooler object to a warmer object.

(C) Heat is transferred because the hot toast and the butter are touching.

(D) The transfer of heat will stop when the butter begins to melt.

TEKS 4.6A

15 Heat must flow to cause a material to change its temperature. Which action will change an ice cube's temperature in the shortest amount of time?

(A) placing the ice cube in a freezer

(B) placing the ice cube on a countertop

(C) placing the ice cube in a glass of warm water

(D) placing the ice cube in a pot of boiling water

TEKS 4.6A

16 A student has two metal cups and two foam cups. She places one of each type on a metal plate and one of each type on a foam plate. She then fills each cup with very hot water.

Metal cup

Metal plates

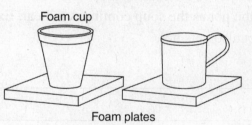
Foam cup

Foam plates

Differentiate between the conductors and insulators shown above. Which cup will lose heat the quickest?

(A) foam cup on foam plate

(B) foam cup on metal plate

(C) metal cup on foam plate

(D) metal cup on metal plate

TEKS 4.6B

17 Darnell needs an insulator to keep liquids hot. He tests how quickly different materials change temperature when they are heated. All materials start at 20 °C and are heated at the same time. He records the temperatures of the materials after 10 minutes and constructs a table to organize the data.

	Material 1	Material 2	Material 3	Material 4
Temperature after 10 min (°C)	49	29	25	37

Which material should he choose as the insulator?

(A) Material 1

(B) Material 2

(C) Material 3

(D) Material 4

TEKS 4.2C, 4.6B

18 Differentiate among forms of energy by identifying the type of energy that is transferred to a pan placed on the glowing burner of an electric stove.

(A) light

(B) heat

(C) electrical

(D) mechanical

TEKS 4.6A

Apply Inquiry and Review the Big Ideas
Write the answers to these questions.

19 Give an example of a heat source in your home. Explain how the heat source transfers heat.

_____

_____

TEKS 4.6A, 4.6B

20 A farmer is planning to build a barn. The walls of the barn can be either wood or metal. Which is likely to be warmer in the winter and cooler in the summer? Why?

_____

_____

TEKS 4.6B

21 Differentiate among forms of energy to identify the energy conversion when a guitar is plugged into an amplifier.

_____

_____

TEKS 4.6A

22 A pan of soup is placed on the stove. The burner is turned on and the soup begins to warm. A metal spoon is used to stir the soup and is left in the pot as the soup continues to heat. Explain why the part of the spoon that sticks above the pot also gets hot.

_____

_____

TEKS 4.6A, 4.6B

23 Examine the data in the chart. Which numeral gives the temperature of water that was initially heated to 100 °C but was then poured into a bowl containing four ice cubes?

Test	°C
A	102
B	107
C	89

⓪⓪⓪
①①①
②②②
③③③
④④④
⑤⑤⑤
⑥⑥⑥
⑦⑦⑦
⑧⑧⑧
⑨⑨⑨

TEKS 4.5A

Forms of Energy

Materials

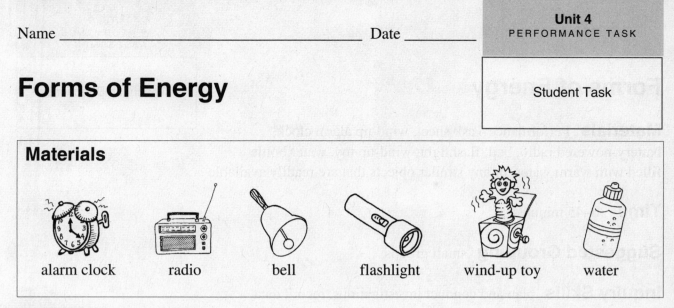

alarm clock   radio   bell   flashlight   wind-up toy   water

Procedure

 1 Work as a group to quickly review the properties of mechanical, sound, electrical, light, and heat/thermal energy.

2 Plan a descriptive investigation of the forms of energy used by common objects. Make a list of questions to guide your inquiry. For example, you might ask, How does the object work? Does the object use more than one form of energy? Think of additional questions that can help you differentiate among forms of energy.

_____

_____

_____

3 Your teacher will provide objects similar to the ones shown above. Select one of the objects. Examine the object to find answers to your questions. Test how the object works. What inferences can you make about the forms of energy based on the answers to your questions and what you observe? Use descriptive words to record your findings.

_____

_____

_____

_____

4 Communicate your findings orally to the class. Compare your data with the data collected by other groups. As a class, interpret the patterns to create a reasonable explanation of how to differentiate among forms of energy.

Forms of Energy

Materials Performance Task sheet, wind-up alarm clock, battery-powered radio, bell, flashlight, wind-up toy, water bottle filled with warm water, or any similar objects that are readily available

Time 30–45 minutes

Suggested Grouping small groups

Inquiry Skills plan and conduct investigations, record data

Preparation Hints Gather a variety of the suggested objects. Each group will need one object to investigate. Make sure that the objects represent mechanical, sound, electrical, light, and heat/thermal energy.

Introduce the Task Explain that in this task, students will plan and conduct a descriptive investigation designed to differentiate forms of energy. List the forms of energy on the board. Point to a ceiling light in the room. Have students identify the forms of energy (electrical, light). Point to another object in the room and repeat the exercise.

Promote Discussion Have each group communicate their findings orally. Help students compare the data and interpret the patterns. Have students use examples from their observations to explain ways to differentiate among forms of energy.

Scoring Rubric

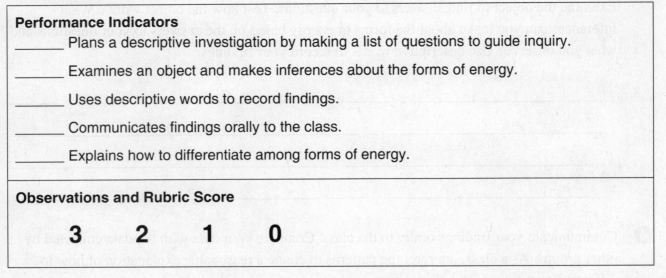

Performance Indicators

_____ Plans a descriptive investigation by making a list of questions to guide inquiry.

_____ Examines an object and makes inferences about the forms of energy.

_____ Uses descriptive words to record findings.

_____ Communicates findings orally to the class.

_____ Explains how to differentiate among forms of energy.

Observations and Rubric Score

3   2   1   0

What Is an Electric Circuit?

❶ Autumn wants to make an electric circuit. She wants to demonstrate that electricity travels in a closed path. She gathers the items shown below.

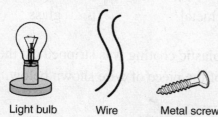

Light bulb   Wire   Metal screw

What additional item does Autumn need to make a complete circuit?

- Ⓐ a battery
- Ⓑ a switch
- Ⓒ an insulator
- Ⓓ a conductor

❷ Differentiate between conductors and insulators. Which of the following items would allow a circuit to work?

- Ⓐ glass bead
- Ⓑ metal coin
- Ⓒ plastic straw
- Ⓓ wooden toothpick

❸ Lori wants to know if a wooden craft stick can act as a conductor to close a circuit that turns on a light bulb. She implements a descriptive investigation by setting up a wooden stick as the switch and records her data. Which observation did she record?

- Ⓐ The bulb remains unlit.
- Ⓑ The bulb becomes brighter.
- Ⓒ The bulb flickers on and off.
- Ⓓ The bulb lights for 2 seconds.

❹ Jackson arranges the parts of a circuit as shown below.

Where should he put a piece of wire in order to complete the circuit to demonstrate that electricity travels in a closed path?

- Ⓐ between the top of the paper clip and the bottom of the light bulb
- Ⓑ between the top of the battery and the bottom of the light bulb
- Ⓒ between the top of the paper clip and the bottom of the battery
- Ⓓ between the top of the battery and the top of the paper clip

❺ Oscar makes an electric circuit that has a closed switch as one of its parts to demonstrate that electricity travels in a closed path. The diagram below shows the circuit that he makes.

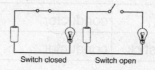

Switch closed   Switch open

He changes the switch to open and records the results using descriptive words. What words did Oscar record?

- Ⓐ It is duller.
- Ⓑ It is brighter.
- Ⓒ It stops glowing.
- Ⓓ It burns the wire.

What Are Electric Circuits, Conductors, and Insulators?

① The electric circuit below consists of a battery, a switch, and three light bulbs.

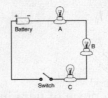

What type of circuit is shown in the diagram?

(A) mechanical circuit

(B) series circuit

(C) magnetic circuit

(D) parallel circuit

② Jennifer looked at a group of objects and classified them as electrical conductors or insulators. She constructed the chart below to differentiate between conductors and insulators.

Object	Classification
glass bead	insulator
plastic plate	insulator
aluminum foil	conductor
silver bracelet	conductor
wooden craft stick	conductor

How many objects are classified correctly?

(A) 0

(B) 1

(C) 2

(D) 4

③ Conductors help electricity move when a closed path creates an electric circuit. Identify the electrical conductor.

(A) wood   (C) plastic

(B) metal   (D) glass

④ The plastic coating was stripped off the end of the piece of wire shown below.

Copper wire

Differentiate between conductors and insulators. Why must the plastic be removed before this wire is used in an electric circuit?

(A) so the wire can be bent and fit into the circuit

(B) to prevent the circuit from becoming overloaded

(C) because the plastic makes the wire too thick to use in a circuit

(D) so electric current can pass between the copper and the rest of the circuit

⑤ Valentina wants to demonstrate that electricity travels in a closed path, creating an electric circuit. Which list contains all the materials she needs for her circuit?

(A) wire, ruler, switch, battery

(B) string, buzzer, battery, switch

(C) buzzer, wire, switch, light bulb

(D) battery, wire, light bulb, switch

How Do We Use Electricity?

1 The picture below shows a device made of a battery, a nail, and a long piece of copper wire. It converts electrical energy into a different form of energy.

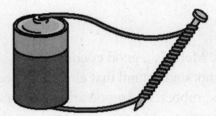

Which term below describes the device in the picture?

Ⓐ electric switch

Ⓑ electromagnet

Ⓒ electric motor

Ⓓ electric generator

2 You have been asked to design an experiment to test the effect of magnetism on objects. You decide to explore an electromagnetic field. Which of the items would you need to make an electromagnet?

Ⓐ battery, copper wire, magnet, glass jar, foam insulation

Ⓑ plastic straw, copper wire, magnet, thumb tack, glass jar

Ⓒ copper wire, iron nail, foam insulation, glass straw, staples

Ⓓ iron nail, battery, copper wire, magnetic object such as a paper clip

3 Which is an example of an electromagnet?

Ⓐ copper wire   Ⓒ electric bell

Ⓑ closed circuit   Ⓓ bar magnet

4 Camila designs an experiment to test the effect of magnetism on objects. She wraps the magnet with a copper wire. She moves the magnet inside the wire coil, producing an electric current.

Movement of magnet

Coil

In her exploration of the electromagnetic field, what discovery will Camila make about the electric current if the magnet no longer moves inside the coil?

Ⓐ It will stop flowing.

Ⓑ It will continue to flow as it did.

Ⓒ It will flow in the opposite direction.

Ⓓ It will start to flow in the magnet instead of the wire.

5 What does an electromagnet produce?

Ⓐ an open circuit

Ⓑ an electromagnetic field

Ⓒ a magnet out of plastic wire

Ⓓ two electric currents of equal strength

Electricity and Circuits

TEKS DOK Skill Builder

Use the following practice questions to help students build their comprehension skills for one
TEKS at increasing depths of knowledge. The teacher notes below provide answers and
strategies for diagnosing incorrect responses.

4.6C

Level 1: Recall and Reproduction

1. C; The metal paper clip would work best to close the circuit. Metal is a good conductor of
    electricity. **Diagnose:** Students who miss this question may not understand that electricity needs
    a circuit to travel along and metal is a good conductor. Glass, rubber, and wood are insulators.
    They would not help electricity move along a circuit. If students need further support, have them
    review the discussion of circuits in the Student Edition or digital lesson.

Level 2: Skills and Concepts

2. A; The switch needs to be closed to complete the circuit. **Diagnose:** Students who miss this
    question have not yet mastered the concept that electricity will flow only through a closed
    circuit. Have students trace the path of the wire. Ask them what will happen when the electricity
    reaches the switch. If students suggest that the electricity will jump the gap, have them review
    the discussion of closed circuits in the Student Edition or digital lesson.

Level 3: Strategic Thinking

3. A; Only Bulb 2 will go out. The circuit can be completed for the other two bulbs. **Diagnose:**
    Students who miss this question may be confused by the fact that the first switch is being
    opened. They may think that this breaks all of the circuits. Help them see that only the circuit to
    Bulb 2 has been opened. Other switches complete the circuit for the other two bulbs. If students
    still do not understand, have them review the discussion of closed circuits in the Student Edition
    or digital lesson.

Electricity and Circuits

Choose the letter of the best answer.

TEKS 4.6C

1 Which of the following items would work best to close a circuit?

- Ⓐ a rubber band
- Ⓑ a glass marble
- Ⓒ a metal paper clip
- Ⓓ a wooden chopstick

2 Look at the circuit below.

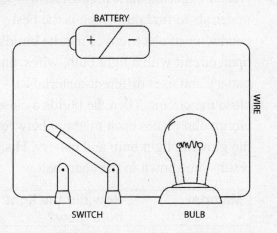

What needs to happen in order for the battery to light the bulb?

- Ⓐ The switch needs to be closed.
- Ⓑ The wire needs to be insulated.
- Ⓒ The battery needs to be charged.
- Ⓓ The bulb needs to be moved to the other side of the switch.

3 Look at the circuit below.

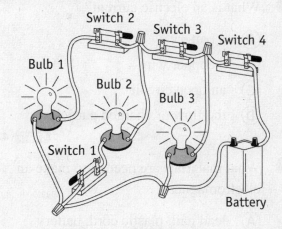

What will happen if Switch 1 is opened?

- Ⓐ Bulb 2 will go out.
- Ⓑ Bulbs 1 and 2 will go out.
- Ⓒ Bulbs 2 and 3 will go out.
- Ⓓ All of the bulbs will go out.

Electricity and Circuits

Vocabulary and Concepts

1 What is an electric current?

Ⓐ a battery

Ⓑ a copper wire

Ⓒ an open circuit

Ⓓ the flow of charged particles

TEKS 4.6C

2 What materials are needed to make an electromagnet?

Ⓐ lead nail, plastic cord, battery

Ⓑ an energy source, wire, magnet

Ⓒ copper wire, iron nail, battery

Ⓓ magnet, nylon thread, switch

TEKS 4.6C

3 When new communities are developed, bringing power to the community is very important. Connect science concepts with science careers. Which of the following careers includes a thorough understanding of electricity and circuits?

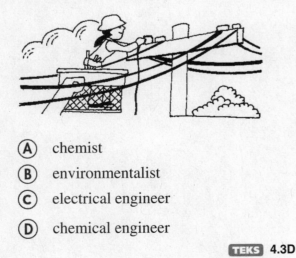

Ⓐ chemist

Ⓑ environmentalist

Ⓒ electrical engineer

Ⓓ chemical engineer

TEKS 4.3D

4 Differentiate between conductors and insulators. Which of the following materials is a conductor?

Ⓐ a toothpick

Ⓑ a plastic ruler

Ⓒ a rubber band

Ⓓ a paper clip

TEKS 4.6B

5 Hector experiments with different materials to find out which is the best conductor of electricity. First, he builds an open circuit with a light bulb, wires, and a battery and uses different materials to close the circuit. Then, he builds a closed circuit and places each material between the glowing light bulb and battery. His results are shown in the chart below.

Material	How did the light bulb glow?
foam	very dim
plastic	dim
aluminum	bright
silver	very bright

Based on what you can infer from Hector's data, which material should he choose as a conductor?

Ⓐ silver   Ⓒ foam

Ⓑ plastic   Ⓓ aluminum

TEKS 4.2B, 4.6B

6 Conservation of energy reduces the amount of electricity that needs to be generated. Which of these makes an informed choice in the use and conservation of natural resources used to generate electricity?

(A) Turn the television sound down so it is not as loud.

(B) Replace compact fluorescent light bulbs with incandescent light bulbs.

(C) Turn off the lights in a room when you leave it or when the lights are not needed.

(D) Cool the house by leaving the refrigerator door open instead of using an air conditioner.

TEKS 4.1B

7 Darnell wants to demonstrate that electricity travels in a closed path. He creates a list of symbols used for the parts of the circuit diagram shown below.

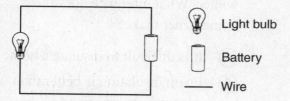

Light bulb

Battery

—— Wire

What is the purpose of the battery in the circuit?

(A) to use the electric current

(B) to connect the components

(C) to provide a source of energy

(D) to slow the flow of electricity

TEKS 4.6C

8 Chris has a circuit made up of a battery, a light bulb, some wires, and a metal rod as a switch. He wants to explore the electromagnetic field so he replaces the metal rod with a wooden rod. When Chris closes the new switch, what will he observe?

(A) unlit bulb

(B) flashing bulb

(C) warmer bulb

(D) brighter bulb

TEKS 4.6B

9 Sarah wants to convert electrical energy into a different form of energy. She builds a device by wrapping a long piece of copper wire around a nail and attaching both ends of the wire to a battery. Which term describes the device she has made?

(A) electric switch

(B) electromagnet

(C) electric motor

(D) electric generator

TEKS 4.6C

⑩ Maria wants to create an electric circuit. She draws the following diagram and builds the circuit.

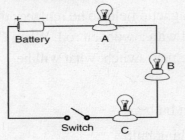

What will happen if the switch is closed?

Ⓐ The battery will recharge.

Ⓑ Bulbs A, B, and C will go out.

Ⓒ Bulbs A, B, and C will light up.

Ⓓ Charges will stop flowing.

TEKS 4.6C

⑪ Look at the drawing below. It needs to be labeled. Differentiate between conductors and insulators. Where should the word *conductor* be written on the drawing?

Ⓐ on the ceramic outlet cover

Ⓑ on the metal prongs

Ⓒ on the rubber electrical cord

Ⓓ on the plastic outlet face

TEKS 4.6B

⑫ Look at the labeled drawing below.

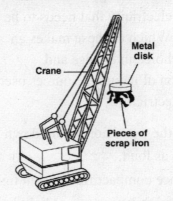

Which word best describes the metal disk?

Ⓐ battery   Ⓒ engine

Ⓑ electromagnet   Ⓓ motor

TEKS 4.6C

⑬ A homeowner is deciding which insulating material to put into his attic. He contacts several other homeowners. Most say that they installed foam insulation instead of fiberglass and that their homes seem to stay warmer in the winter. What inference does the homeowner make?

Ⓐ It is difficult to insulate a home.

Ⓑ Foam insulation is better than fiberglass insulation.

Ⓒ Foam and fiberglass do about the same job of insulating.

Ⓓ All homeowners should consider insulating their homes with foam.

TEKS 4.6B

14 Connect science concepts with science careers. Which of the following careers helps homeowners improve energy efficiency in their homes by improving the home's wiring?

(A) electrician

(C) custodian

(B) civil engineer

(D) line worker

TEKS 4.3D

15 Which of the following describes how people can make informed choices about the use and conservation of natural resources?

(A) Recycle glass, cans, and newspapers.

(B) Ride in a car instead of riding a bicycle.

(C) Leave the lights on at all times instead of turning them off and on.

(D) Allow the water to run when washing dishes to save wear and tear on the faucet.

TEKS 4.1B

16 Sophia tries to build an electric circuit using a battery, a light bulb, a paper clip, and copper wire. She wants to demonstrate that electricity in an electric circuit travels in a closed path. The diagram below shows what she builds.

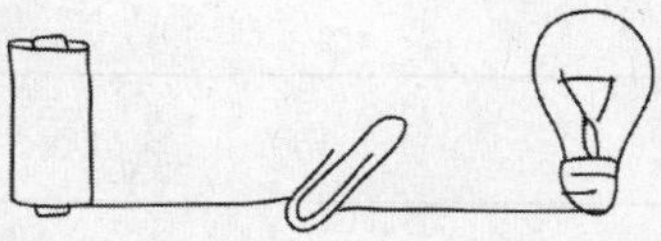

Which statement explains the problem with her circuit?

(A) The circuit lacks an energy source.

(B) The circuit is not a complete loop.

(C) The light bulb uses the electric current.

(D) The paper clip stops the electric current.

TEKS 4.6C

Name ________________________ Date __________

Apply Inquiry and Review the Big Ideas

Write the answers to these questions.

17. A circuit is made up of a battery, a small fan, a metal paper clip, and copper wire. When the metal paper clip is replaced with a plastic paper clip, the fan stops spinning. Differentiate between conductors and insulators. What can you conclude about the plastic paper clip?

____

____

TEKS 4.6B

18. Explain one way you can conserve the natural resources used to produce electricity.

____

____

TEKS 4.1B

19. Why must a conductor be used as a switch in a closed circuit?

____

____

TEKS 4.6C

20. Identify the materials you would need and explain your design for a simple electromagnet.

____

____

____

TEKS 4.6C

21. In the electric circuit below, light bulbs are placed at A, B, and C. How many bulbs will light when the switch is closed?

		.
0	0	0
1	1	1
2	2	2
3	3	3
4	4	4
5	5	5
6	6	6
7	7	7
8	8	8
9	9	9

TEKS 4.6C

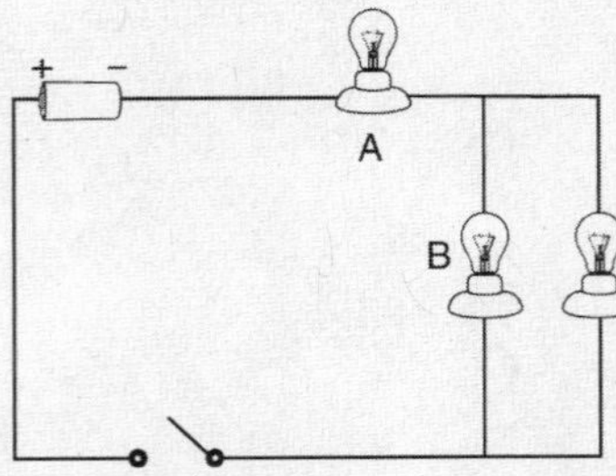

Invent a Battery Tester

Materials

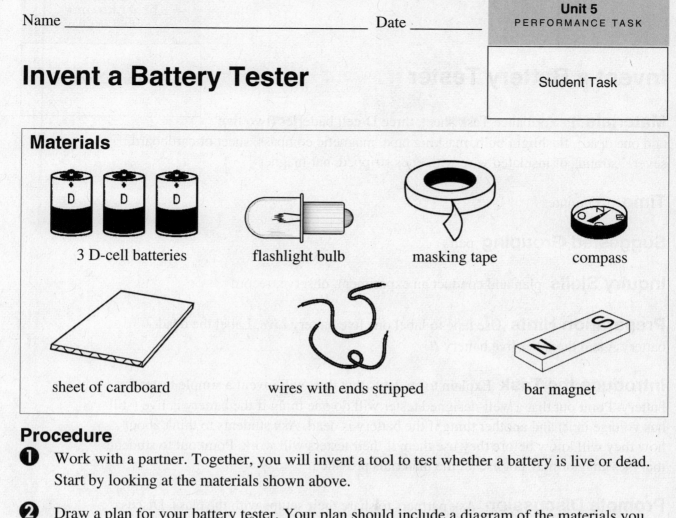

3 D-cell batteries   flashlight bulb   masking tape   compass

sheet of cardboard   wires with ends stripped   bar magnet

Procedure

❶ Work with a partner. Together, you will invent a tool to test whether a battery is live or dead. Start by looking at the materials shown above.

❷ Draw a plan for your battery tester. Your plan should include a diagram of the materials you intend to use and a plan for making sure your tester works before you use it. Remember, electricity travels in a closed path and requires a battery or other energy source to make an electric circuit.

❸ After you have drawn your plan, get the materials you need. Then build your tester. Label each part of your tester.

❹ Test your battery tester by using the D-cell battery labeled *Live*. If your setup does not work, draw up a new design, build it, and test it. Change it until you have a design that works.

❺ When you have a tester that works, use it to test the two batteries labeled *A* and *B*. Describe what your tester does for each battery, and write a conclusion about whether battery *A* and battery *B* are live or dead.

❻ Compare your battery tester and your results with another team's. How are your testers alike? How are they different? Do both testers do the job they are supposed to do?

Invent a Battery Tester

Materials Performance Task sheet, three D-cell batteries (two live and one dead), flashlight bulb, masking tape, magnetic compass, sheet of cardboard, several strands of insulated wire with ends stripped, bar magnet

Time 15 minutes

Suggested Grouping pairs

Inquiry Skills plan and conduct an experiment, observe, record

Preparation Hints Use tape to label one live battery *Live*. Label the dead battery *A* and the other live battery *B*.

Introduce the Task Explain to students that they will invent a simple tester for a battery. Point out that a well-designed tester will do one thing if the battery is live (still has voltage in it) and another thing if the battery is dead. Ask students to think about how they will know before they use them if their testers will work. Point out to students that they may or may not use all the materials provided.

Promote Discussion Ask partners to share their setups with the class. Discuss some ways in which the setups are different. Ask: **Why was it important to use a live battery while building the tester and before using it to test other batteries?** Ask students to think about which physical senses the testers rely on. Ask: **How could you design a battery tester for someone who cannot see?**

Scoring Rubric

Performance Indicators
_____ Draws a plan before building a tester.
_____ Demonstrates that electricity travels in a closed path, requiring a live battery to make an electric circuit.
_____ Builds a tester that correctly identifies battery *A* as dead and battery *B* as live.
_____ Describes the design of a workable tester.
Observations and Rubric Score
3   **2**   **1**   **0**

Name _____ Date _____

What Is Motion?

1 Forces can affect an object's motion. Which of these is a force?

Ⓐ velocity

Ⓒ speed

Ⓑ acceleration

Ⓓ gravity

2 Cars, bicycles, and animals can all be objects in motion. What is it about an object in motion that is constantly changing?

Ⓐ velocity

Ⓒ speed

Ⓑ acceleration

Ⓓ position

3 Lin designed an experiment to test the effect of forces on a toy cart that rolls down a long ramp. She covered the ramp with different materials. The table shows the time she measured for each material.

Ramp surface	Time (sec)
foil	2.2
wood	2.5
carpet	4.1
plastic	2.3

Analyze the data. Which force caused the cart's time to increase on the carpet?

Ⓐ mass

Ⓒ friction

Ⓑ gravity

Ⓓ weight

4 Look at the picture below.

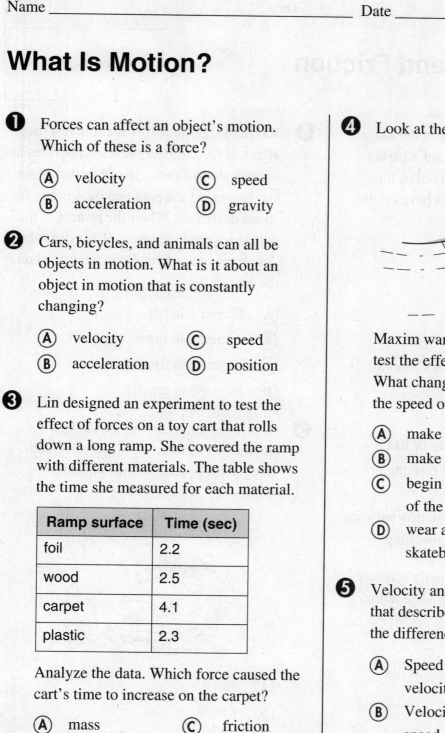

Maxim wants to design an experiment to test the effect of force on the skateboard. What change could he make to increase the speed of the skateboard?

Ⓐ make the ramp less steep

Ⓑ make the ramp as slick as possible

Ⓒ begin skateboarding from the middle of the ramp

Ⓓ wear a heavy backpack while skateboarding on the ramp

5 Velocity and speed are both measurements that describe an object's motion. What is the difference between velocity and speed?

Ⓐ Speed depends on acceleration, but velocity does not.

Ⓑ Velocity depends on direction, but speed does not.

Ⓒ Velocity depends on friction, but speed does not.

Ⓓ Speed depends on velocity, but acceleration does not.

How Do Gravity and Friction Affect Motion?

1 A hot air balloon is floating in the air. A person riding in the balloon's basket throws a heavy bag of sand out of the basket. What effect will this have on the balloon?

(A) decrease in lift

(B) decrease in mass

(C) increase in gravity

(D) increase in friction

2 Friction can affect an object's motion. What is friction?

(A) a unit of the metric system

(B) a unit that is a measure of force

(C) energy in the form of pushing or pulling

(D) a force that opposes motion between two surfaces that are touching

3 Which surface would probably offer the least friction if you were to slide a box across it?

(A) glass

(B) wood

(C) carpet

(D) brick

4 Karyn designs an experiment to test the effect of force on her bicycle. She rides her bicycle along a path. She finds that when she moves off the path and onto grass, her speed decreases. When she returns to the path, her speed increases. What does she determine caused her change in speed on the grass?

(A) decrease in lift

(B) decrease in mass

(C) increase in friction

(D) increase in gravity

5 A bobsled glides across the ice and gradually begins to slow down. Which force acts opposite to the bobsled's motion?

(A) thrust

(B) weight

(C) gravity

(D) friction

Forces and Motion

TEKS DOK Skill Builder

Use the following practice questions to help students build their comprehension skills for one TEKS at increasing depths of knowledge. The teacher notes below provide answers and strategies for diagnosing incorrect responses.

4.6D

Level 1: Recall and Reproduction

1. A; Using a wheeled cart will require the least amount of force because the cart produces the least amount of friction. **Diagnose:** Students who miss this question may not be considering the effects of friction. Ask students to describe each picture. Have them consider which surface would produce the least amount of friction. Lead them to understand that the wheels are round and make the least amount of contact with the ground. This reduces friction. The sheet provides a slick surface, which will reduce friction somewhat. Pushing on the grass or ground will produce the most friction because the surfaces are rough. If students need further support, have them review the discussion of friction in the Student Edition or digital lesson.

Level 2: Skills and Concepts

2. C; The experiment is designed to measure the effects of friction on the amount of force needed to move an object. **Diagnose:** Ask students to describe what they see. They should note the box of sand, the spring scale, the sandpaper, and the wax paper. Ask students what the spring scale is designed to measure (force). Point out the sandpaper and wax paper and ask students about the surface of each. They should note that the sandpaper is rough and the wax paper is smooth and slick. Students who miss this question may have failed to correctly identify the elements in the picture or were unable to infer how they would be used. Help students see that the experiment will involve pulling the box over each of the surfaces to compare the force needed. You may wish to have students review the discussion of friction in the Student Edition or digital lesson.

Level 3: Strategic Thinking

3. D; Jennifer is most likely testing whether the angle and design of a ramp affects the speed and distance a marble travels. **Diagnose:** Students who miss this question may not be focusing on Jennifer's interest in how forces affect motion. Have students reread the question carefully and list the main idea. Also have students examine the pictures. This should help them eliminate all but the correct answer. Discuss how the two ramp designs enable Jennifer to test the effects of gravity and friction on acceleration. If this is difficult for students to see, have them review the discussions of gravity, friction, and acceleration in the Student Edition or digital lesson.

Forces and Motion

Choose the letter of the best answer.

❶ Luke and Sarah are conducting an experiment on friction.

Which method of moving the crate will require the least amount of force?

Ⓐ 1   Ⓒ 3

Ⓑ 2   Ⓓ 4

❷ Look at the picture below.

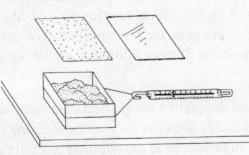

What is this experiment designed to test?

Ⓐ gravity

Ⓑ weight

Ⓒ friction

Ⓓ acceleration

❸ Jennifer is interested in how force affects motion. She has designed an experiment that uses a book, ruler, curved ramp, and marble in the manner shown below.

Which of the following experiments do you think she is most likely conducting?

Ⓐ She is testing which ramp design is the strongest.

Ⓑ She is testing how push and pull factors affect friction.

Ⓒ She is testing the effects of magnetism on the acceleration of a marble on a steep surface.

Ⓓ She is testing whether the angle and design of a ramp affects the speed and distance a marble travels.

Forces and Motion

Vocabulary and Concepts

1 Velocity is a measurement related to motion. What is velocity?

- Ⓐ a force that considers the rate at which acceleration changes
- Ⓑ a force that opposes motion between two surfaces that are touching
- Ⓒ a measure of both the speed and direction of a moving object
- Ⓓ a measure of how fast something moves between two points

TEKS 4.6D

2 Which describes friction?

- Ⓐ a unit that is a measure of speed
- Ⓑ a force that works against gravity
- Ⓒ a form of energy that depends on light and heat
- Ⓓ a force that opposes motion between two surfaces that are touching

TEKS 4.6D

3 The speed of which of the following objects is affected by gravity?

- Ⓐ a rock falling off a high cliff
- Ⓑ an airplane flying through the air
- Ⓒ a sailboat gliding across the water
- Ⓓ a marble rolling along the ground

TEKS 4.6D

4 Astronauts design an experiment to test the effect of force on an object. They know that one of the forces we experience on Earth is less on the moon. Which force are the astronauts testing?

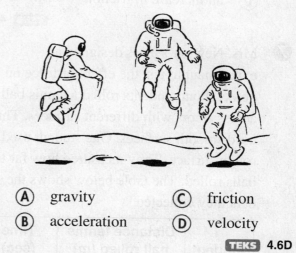

- Ⓐ gravity
- Ⓒ friction
- Ⓑ acceleration
- Ⓓ velocity

TEKS 4.6D

5 A bus driving on the road during the winter drives onto an icy spot and starts to slide. A decrease in which of the following forces causes the bus to slide?

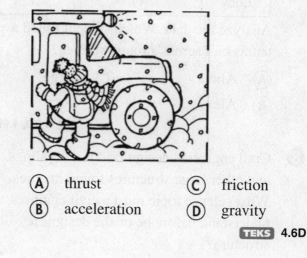

- Ⓐ thrust
- Ⓒ friction
- Ⓑ acceleration
- Ⓓ gravity

TEKS 4.6D

6 A car traveling down a road approaches a red light. The driver pushes the car's brakes and the car slows to a stop. What causes the car's speed to change?

Ⓐ a decrease in velocity

Ⓑ an increase in velocity

Ⓒ a decrease in friction

Ⓓ an increase in friction

TEKS 4.6D

7 Mrs. Newton's class designed an experiment to test the effect of force on an object. Four students rolled a tennis ball across floors with different surfaces. Three used smooth surfaces. One student used a rough surface. They measured how far the balls rolled. The table below shows the data they collected.

Student	Distance tennis ball rolled (m)	Time (sec)
Alex	16	2
Alicia	18	3
Jorge	5	3
Lucy	17	5

Analyze the data. Which student rolled a tennis ball across a rough surface?

Ⓐ Alicia   Ⓒ Jorge

Ⓑ Alex   Ⓓ Lucy

TEKS 4.2D, 4.6D

8 Civil engineers design bridges, buildings, and other large structures found in cities. What science topic must a civil engineer understand before he or she designs a structure?

Ⓐ plants   Ⓒ electricity

Ⓑ forces   Ⓓ geography

TEKS 4.3D

9 Lukas designed an experiment to investigate forces and motion. The table shows the distances and times a ball rolled during his investigation. For each trial, the ball started from rest and a force caused it to move.

Motion of the Ball

Trial	Time (sec)	Distance (m)
1	3	12
2	6	18
3	8	16
4	3	6

Analyze the data. During which trial did the greatest force cause the ball to move?

Ⓐ Trial 1   Ⓒ Trial 3

Ⓑ Trial 2   Ⓓ Trial 4

TEKS 4.2D, 4.6D

10 Bodhi designed an experiment to study motion. He used the measured data he collected about the distance a toy car traveled over time to make this graph.

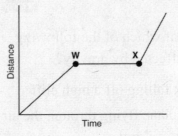

Analyze the pattern shown in the graph. What did Bodhi do to the car between points W and X? 4.2D, 4.6D

Ⓐ He slowed it down.

Ⓑ He made it accelerate.

Ⓒ He put it on a steep incline.

Ⓓ He stopped it from moving.

TEKS 4.2D, 4.6D

11 Jho designs an experiment to test force and motion using a slingshot. He loads a ball into the rubber band of the slingshot as shown in the picture below. Then he tests how far the ball travels.

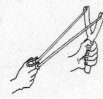

What can Jho do to make the ball travel farthest?

(A) use a heavier ball and pull it back a shorter distance

(B) use a heavier ball and pull it back farther

(C) use a lighter ball and pull it back a shorter distance

(D) use a lighter ball and pull it back farther

TEKS 4.6D

12 Carla designed an experiment to test velocity. She made the table below to analyze her data.

Object	Distance (m)	Time (sec)
A	13	3
B	9	4
C	22	7

What important information is missing from Carla's data table?

(A) the total distance the object traveled

(B) the direction the object traveled

(C) the total time taken to travel the distance

(D) the time taken to complete the experiment

TEKS 4.2D, 4.6D

13 Luis is using toy cars to investigate speed. He is changing the length and shape of the track to see the effects on speed. What change could he make to the investigation to make a car go faster?

(A) make the car as heavy as possible

(B) make the track as rough as possible

(C) make the end of the track higher than the beginning

(D) make the beginning of the track higher than the end

TEKS 4.6D

14 Keesha designs an experiment to test the effect of force on the motion of a ball. She uses a rubber band wrapped around the legs of a chair to launch the ball. She discovers that the farther she pulls back with the rubber band, the faster the ball travels. Which conclusion should she draw?

(A) Increasing the weight of a moving object will increase its speed.

(B) Increasing the distance an object travels will increase its speed.

(C) Increasing the force applied to a moving object will increase its speed.

(D) Increasing the friction on a moving object will increase its speed.

TEKS 4.6D

15 Connect science concepts with science careers. Erica is very interested in forces and motion. In particular, she is interested in how forces and motion affect the planets in the solar system. What career might Erica like?

- (A) physicist
- (B) botanist
- (C) biologist
- (D) chemist

TEKS 4.3D

16 Devin wants to design an experiment to test the effect of force on an object. Which of these should he test to investigate the effect of magnetism?

- (A) the speed of a car moving downhill
- (B) the ability to move a paper clip on a piece of paper without touching the paper or the paper clip
- (C) the time it takes a feather and a tennis ball to fall from a height of six meters
- (D) the behavior of an object that is rolling across a rough surface

TEKS 4.6D

17 Which career includes working with machines that move earth and requires an understanding of forces and motion?

- (A) biologist
- (B) engineer
- (C) psychologist
- (D) meteorologist

TEKS 4.6D

18 Luce wants to test the force of gravity. He sets up the investigation below.

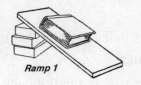

Ramp 1   Ramp 2

Besides gravity, what other force is Luce testing?

- (A) magnetism
- (B) velocity
- (C) friction
- (D) acceleration

TEKS 4.6D

Apply Inquiry and Review the Big Ideas

Write the answers to these questions.

19 Compare and contrast speed and velocity.

_____

_____

TEKS 4.6D

20 A group of engineers has designed a high-speed train that will travel from New York to Indianapolis. Think about gravity, friction, and magnetism. Identify how two of these forces could act on the train at all times.

_____

_____

TEKS 4.6D

21 What is the difference between gravity and friction?

_____

_____

TEKS 4.6D

22 You want to design a new skateboard ramp to test how forces affect a skateboarder's motion. What two skateboard ramp designs might you test? What would you be testing in each skateboard ramp design?

_____

_____

TEKS 4.6D

23 The table below shows the initial speed of identical balls kicked by three soccer players. Fill in the speed, in m/sec, of the ball kicked with the greatest force.

Player	Speed (m/sec)
Will	19
Corey	15
Teri	17

TEKS 4.2D, 4.6D

Bobsled Races

Materials

oil

petroleum jelly

water in spray bottle

heavy bolt

stack of books

metric ruler

Procedure

Using the heavy bolt for a bobsled, compare three surfaces to test the effect of friction on an object. Your teacher will provide each team with three tracks that are lined with aluminum foil.

❶ Lightly cover each of the tracks with a different material (oil, petroleum jelly, or water).

❷ Predict which surface will allow the bobsled to travel the farthest.

❸ Test your prediction. Prop up the tracks, one at a time, on the stack of books. Give the same push to the bobsled on each track.

❹ Record the distances in the data table. Analyze and evaluate the data. Was your prediction correct?

Track	Distance traveled from top of ramp
Track with oil	
Track with petroleum jelly	
Track with water	

Bobsled Races

Materials Performance Task sheets, oil, petroleum jelly, water in spray bottles, heavy bolts, stacks of books, metric rulers, tracks made by the teacher in advance

Time 30 minutes

Suggested Grouping groups of three or four

Inquiry Skills predict, experiment, observe, record data

Preparation Hints Make three tracks for each group of students. First, cut identical strips of poster board; the strips should be about 8 cm wide and 60–90 cm long. Cover each strip with aluminum foil, folding the foil around the edges. Fold up the long sides of each strip about 2 cm to keep the bobsled from falling off. Alternatively, you may wish to have students construct the bobsled tracks. Make sure there is enough space in the room for students to conduct their trials.

Introduce the Task Begin the activity by asking students what kinds of things help reduce friction (oil, smooth ice). Then have students name things that make more friction (bumpy ice, other rough surfaces). Tell students that they will conduct an investigation to see what kind of surface allows a small, heavy object—their bolt "bobsled"—to travel the farthest.

Promote Discussion When students finish, have the groups compare results. Are they the same or different? If different, can students explain why? Were their predictions correct?

Scoring Rubric

Performance Indicators
_____ Coats each track surface with one material: oil, petroleum jelly, or water.
_____ Measures distance accurately with a metric ruler.
_____ Records data in the table.
_____ Compares results with prediction.

Observations and Rubric Score
3   2   1   0

What Are Natural Resources?

❶ Which of the following would you classify as two of Earth's renewable resources?

(A) coal and air

(B) plants and water

(C) oil and natural gas

(D) animals and natural gas

❷ Which of the following would you classify as two of Earth's nonrenewable resources?

(A) coal and air

(B) plants and water

(C) oil and natural gas

(D) animals and natural gas

❸ Identify one of Earth's nonrenewable resources found in rock outcrops like these.

(A) air

(B) coal

(C) water

(D) plants

❹ Identify which of Earth's renewable resources moves this turbine.

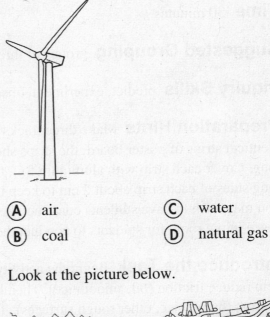

(A) air

(B) coal

(C) water

(D) natural gas

❺ Look at the picture below.

Identify one of Earth's renewable resources missing from this picture.

(A) oil

(B) water

(C) plants

(D) animals

How Do Weathering and Erosion Shape Earth's Surface?

❶ Wind can cause erosion. Identify which of the following choices is an example of a slow change to Earth's surface caused by erosion from wind.

- (A) tides
- (B) moraines
- (C) sand dunes
- (D) alluvial fans

❷ There is a relationship between wind and slow changes to Earth's surface. Given this relationship, identify which landform is caused by deposition from wind.

- (A) sand dune
- (B) forest
- (C) canyon
- (D) mountain

❸ Observe the picture of the canyon below.

What is the primary cause of this slow change to Earth's surface?

- (A) erosion from wind
- (B) erosion from water
- (C) deposition from wind
- (D) deposition from water

❹ The water in a fast-moving river causes rocks to bump and scrape against one another. Identify which slow change to Earth's surface this weathering from water will cause.

- (A) The rocks will get larger.
- (B) The rocks will get heavier.
- (C) The rocks will get sharper.
- (D) The rocks will get smaller.

❺ Observe the moraines in the picture of the glacial valley below.

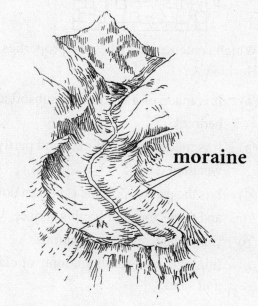

moraine

What caused this slow change to Earth's surface?

- (A) erosion from ice
- (B) erosion from wind
- (C) deposition from ice
- (D) deposition from wind

How Do Soils Form?

1 What takes place first in the process of soil formation?

- (A) decomposition
- (C) pressure
- (B) weathering
- (D) heat

2 This picture shows a soil profile.

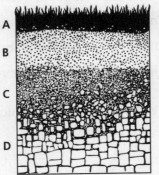

Which sentence describes the properties of Horizon A?

- (A) It is made of a mixture of subsoil and bedrock.
- (B) It is made mostly of clay and partly weathered rock.
- (C) It is the parent rock that is broken down and forms much of Earth's surface.
- (D) It is a dark mixture of humus, minerals, and small amounts of clay and sand.

3 What is the main way scientists group soils?

- (A) according to how well they support plant growth
- (B) according to the amount of sand, silt, and clay they contain
- (C) according to the amount of organic materials present in a sample
- (D) according to whether they contain topsoil or only subsoil

4 Megan is examining the properties of soils. She discovers that clay-rich soils are less able than some other soils to support the growth of plants. Which properties of clay-rich soil cause this lessened ability to support the growth of plants?

- (A) Clay-rich soil contains too much humus and holds water, which can cause plants to drown.
- (B) Clay-rich soil does not retain water well, so plants may not be able to survive a dry period.
- (C) The particles in clay-rich soil are closely packed, so the roots of many plants are not able to break through.
- (D) Clay-rich soil contains large conglomerate rocks that make it difficult for the roots of plants to take hold.

5 The ability to hold water is one of the properties of soils. Some soils retain water better than others. Charlie is examining different soils. Which soil does he find has the least capacity to retain water?

- (A) sandy soil
- (B) loamy soil
- (C) clay-rich soil
- (D) humus-rich soil

How Can We Examine Properties of Soil?

1 Sabrina knows that soil texture is determined by the size of the soil particles. Sand has the largest particles, followed by silt and then clay. She sets up an observational test to determine texture by the feel of the soil, using four soil samples:

- Sample 1: mostly sand with some silt and clay
- Sample 2: mostly silt with some sand and clay
- Sample 3: mostly clay
- Sample 4: a balance of sand, silt, and clay

Which soil sample will have the finest texture?

Ⓐ Sample 1   Ⓒ Sample 3
Ⓑ Sample 2   Ⓓ Sample 4

2 Ed is examining soil samples to compare properties. What property of soil could he compare without touching the samples or performing an experiment?

Ⓐ color
Ⓑ mass
Ⓒ capacity to retain water
Ⓓ ability to support the growth of plants

3 Which of the following is not a component of soil?

Ⓐ sand   Ⓒ rocks
Ⓑ roots   Ⓓ humus

4 Yvette is designing an experiment to test which soil is best for growing tomato plants. Which of the following properties is the most important for her to examine?

Ⓐ color of the soil
Ⓑ smell of the soil
Ⓒ how fast the soil erodes
Ⓓ how the soil holds water

5 Maxim places a sample of soil in a jar, fills the jar with water, and puts a lid on tightly. He shakes the mixture and then lets it sit overnight. The next day, the soil has settled into layers.

What property of soil is Maxim examining?

Ⓐ color
Ⓑ texture
Ⓒ capacity to retain water
Ⓓ ability to support the growth of plants

Earth's Surface

TEKS DOK Skill Builder

Use the following practice questions to help students build their comprehension skills for one TEKS at increasing depths of knowledge. The teacher notes below provide answers and strategies for diagnosing incorrect responses.

4.7B

Level 1: Recall and Reproduction

1. C; Weathering is the process of breaking down rock by wind, water, and ice. **Diagnose:** Students who miss this question may not recall the definitions of the different processes. They may also have missed the focus of the question. Ask students to read the question aloud and tell you the main idea (the breaking down of rock). Then ask them to define *erosion, deposition,* and *weathering.* Ask them what the word *sediment* means. Then explain that sedimentation results from weathering and erosion. Have students who missed this question review the discussion of weathering in the Student Edition or digital lesson.

Level 2: Skills and Concepts

2. B; A delta forms at the mouth of a river through the process of deposition. **Diagnose:** To answer this question correctly, students must know the definition of *deposition* and apply it to the example. To do this, they must also know what a delta is. Ask students to define *deposition.* Then ask them what a delta is. Discuss how deltas form. Lead students to understand that the other answer choices involve weathering and erosion. Have students who missed this question review the discussion of deposition in the Student Edition or digital lesson.

Level 3: Strategic Thinking

3. A; The homeowners should plant grass to stop the erosion. **Diagnose:** To answer this question correctly, students must understand the concept of erosion, analyze the picture to determine the problem, and consider how the problem can be solved. Students who miss this question are having difficulty with one of these steps. Ask students to define *erosion.* Then have them point out the example of erosion in the picture. Talk about what caused the erosion. Then ask students which of the answer choices might help keep the soil from washing away when it rains. Students who are unsure of the definition of *erosion* should review the discussion in the Student Edition or digital lesson.

Earth's Surface

Choose the letter of the best answer.

TEKS 4.7B

❶ The breaking down of rock by wind, water, and ice is an example of which slow process that changes Earth's surface?

Ⓐ erosion

Ⓑ deposition

Ⓒ weathering

Ⓓ sedimentation

❷ Which of the following is an example of deposition?

Ⓐ Water and wind shape a rock.

Ⓑ A delta forms at the mouth of a river.

Ⓒ Ice breaks apart the rocks on the side of a cliff.

Ⓓ A river carries away rocks and soil from a river bank.

❸ The flow of water can cause soil erosion. This picture shows soil erosion caused by rain.

If the homeowners want to stop the process of erosion, what can they do?

Ⓐ plant grass

Ⓑ install a sprinkler

Ⓒ fill the hole with dirt

Ⓓ install a chainlink fence

Earth's Surface

Vocabulary and Concepts

1 Which of the following would you classify as two of Earth's renewable resources?

(A) air and oil

(B) animals and air

(C) oil and natural gas

(D) water and natural gas

TEKS 4.7C

2 Observe the picture of the rock formations below.

Which of the following are causes of this slow change in Earth's surface?

(A) grooving from ice and wind

(B) polishing from water and wind

(C) weathering from wind and water

(D) deposition from water and wind

TEKS 4.7B

3 Which of the following is classified as one of Earth's nonrenewable resources because it takes millions of years to replace?

(A) coal

(B) trees

(C) water

(D) sunlight

TEKS 4.7C

4 Observe the ice splitting the rock below.

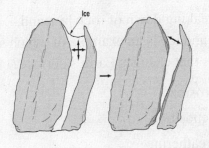

The ice is contributing to slow changes to Earth's surface from—

(A) erosion

(B) polishing

(C) deposition

(D) weathering

TEKS 4.7B

5 Deposition from ice can cause slow changes to Earth's surface. Identify which is an example of deposition from ice.

(A) Ice breaks apart rocks.

(B) Water carries away pieces of floating ice.

(C) Wind carries away pieces of rock and ice.

(D) Glaciers drop rocks and sediment as they melt.

TEKS 4.7B

6 Jorge implements a descriptive investigation to observe the effects of slow changes to Earth's surface. Look at the picture of his investigation below.

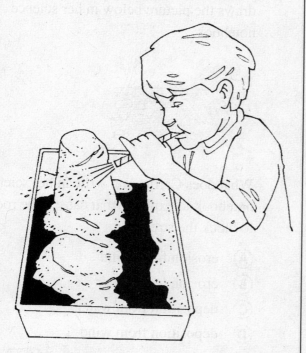

What inference is Jorge trying to make from his investigation?

(A) how wind erosion changes Earth's surface

(B) how water erosion changes Earth's surface

(C) how deposition from wind changes Earth's surface

(D) how deposition from water changes Earth's surface

TEKS 4.2A, 4.7B

7 Identify which of the following are examples of Earth's renewable resources.

(A) oil and water

(B) coal and trees

(C) water and plants

(D) natural gas and sunlight

TEKS 4.7C

8 The farm field shown below is unable to grow crops because of a slow change to Earth's surface. Identify what most likely caused this change.

(A) erosion from ice

(B) erosion from water

(C) deposition from ice

(D) weathering from water

TEKS 4.7B

9 Identify the sentence that tells how weathering from ice causes slow changes to Earth's surface.

(A) A glacier deposits rocks as it moves.

(B) A glacier melts, leaving behind rocks.

(C) A glacier carries away rocks as it moves.

(D) A glacier rubs against rocks as it moves.

TEKS 4.7B

10 The movement of water may have the effect of leaving a solid material behind. Identify which of the following is an example of the slow change to Earth's surface caused by deposition from water.

(A) a sand dune

(B) space in a sinkhole

(C) sand in a river delta

(D) the smoothing of rocks

TEKS 4.7B

11 Deposition from wind is one cause of slow changes to Earth's surface. Observe the pictures below. Identify which picture shows the effects of deposition from wind.

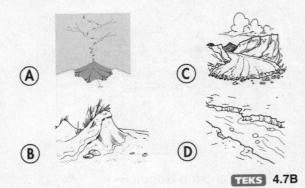

Ⓐ Ⓒ Ⓑ Ⓓ

TEKS 4.7B

12 Identify two of Earth's nonrenewable resources.

Ⓐ coal and water

Ⓑ oil and animals

Ⓒ wind and plants

Ⓓ oil and natural gas

TEKS 4.7C

13 Identify which of the following pictures shows the importance of the conservation of natural resources.

Ⓐ Ⓒ Ⓑ Ⓓ

TEKS 4.1B, 4.7C

14 Carrie Ann has been collecting examples of slow changes to Earth's surface. She observes that rocks have formed a small waterfall in a brook near her home. She draws the picture below in her science notebook.

What does Carrie Ann write in her science notebook to explain what caused the rocks to block the stream?

Ⓐ erosion from wind

Ⓑ erosion from water

Ⓒ deposition from water

Ⓓ deposition from wind

TEKS 4.7B

15 Students are planting a garden. Why would they choose loamy soil for the garden?

Ⓐ because it is young soil and contains many of the nutrients plants need

Ⓑ because it is a mix of sand, silt, and clay and has a rich supply of humus

Ⓒ because it is made up of a great deal of very fine clay sediment and has very little air space

Ⓓ because it is mostly sand, and water passes through it quickly, allowing space for plant roots

TEKS 4.7A

16 Observe the picture of the glacier below.

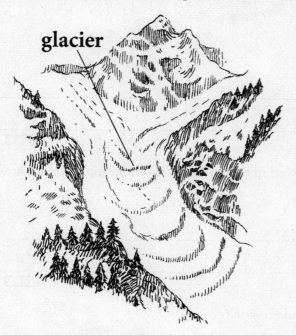

glacier

As a glacier moves down the mountain, it carries with it rocks and other matter. Identify what this slow change to Earth's surface is called.

(A) erosion from ice

(B) erosion from water

(C) deposition from ice

(D) deposition from water

TEKS 4.7B

17 Which correctly identifies the main layers of soil, in order, from closest to Earth's surface to deepest?

(A) topsoil, subsoil, bedrock

(B) subsoil, bedrock, topsoil

(C) humus, topsoil, subsoil

(D) topsoil, subsoil, loam

TEKS 4.7A

18 Rock formations like the one below are examples of slow changes to Earth's surface.

Identify which of the following processes was the primary cause of the shape of the rock formation above.

(A) erosion from water

(B) weathering from rain

(C) deposition from water

(D) weathering from wind

TEKS 4.7B

Name ______________________________ Date __________

Apply Inquiry and Review the Big Idea

Write the answers to these questions.

19 Identify four properties of soil.

____

____

TEKS 4.7A

20 Ice and water are two agents that can be involved in the process of weathering. Explain how freezing and thawing can cause weathering.

____

____

TEKS 4.7B

21 What is the difference between weathering and erosion?

____

____

TEKS 4.7B

22 Mrs. Ruiz gave Sarah a piece of paper. Mrs. Ruiz asked her whether the paper came from a renewable resource or a nonrenewable resource. Sarah said that the paper came from a renewable resource. Was Sarah correct? Explain your answer.

____

____

TEKS 4.7C

23 In one year the soil shown in the picture below erodes 3,600 cm. How many meters, on average, erode each month?

		.
0	0	0
1	1	1
2	2	2
3	3	3
4	4	4
5	5	5
6	6	6
7	7	7
8	8	8
9	9	9

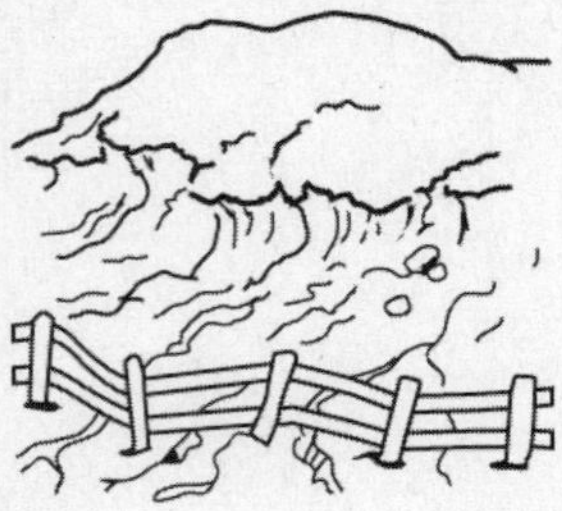

TEKS 4.7B

Student Task

Make a Stream Table Model

Materials

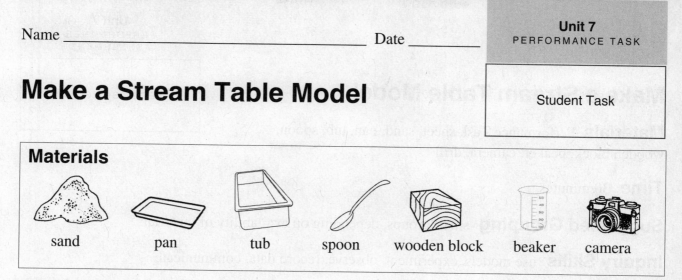

sand   pan   tub   spoon   wooden block   beaker   camera

Procedure

With a group, you are going to make a stream table to model the erosion and deposition caused by water in the natural world.

❶ Place the sand mixture in the pan at the end without holes. Spread out the sand to cover two-thirds of the pan. Leave the end of the pan with the holes empty. Use the spoon to create a shallow S-shaped stream in the sand.

❷ Position the pan on the table or desk so that the end with the holes hangs over the edge. Place the tub below the end of the pan to catch the water that drains through the holes. Use the wooden block to raise the end of the pan that is filled with sand. This will form a slope. Take a photograph of the stream table.

❸ Slowly pour water from the beaker into the beginning of the stream so that the water flows downhill. Vary the rate at which you pour the water. Use the camera to record changes in the stream and surrounding land.

❹ Based on your observations and photographs, communicate the results of your experiment.

_____

_____

_____

❺ Think about the model's accuracy and size. What are the limitations of the model?

_____

_____

_____

Make a Stream Table Model

Materials Performance Task sheet, sand, pan, tub, spoon, wooden block, beaker, camera, drill

Time 30 minutes

Suggested Grouping small groups, depending on availability of materials

Inquiry Skills use models, experiment, observe, record data, communicate

Preparation Hints Prepare a sand mixture that includes coarse, medium grain, and fine sand. Divide the mixture into 2-quart portions for each pan. Drill holes in one end of each pan to allow water to drain. Provide paper towels for each group to use to mop up any spilled water. Have gloves available for anyone who does not want to handle the sand directly. You may want to moisten the sand to make it easier for students to handle.

Introduce the Task Begin the activity by asking students to define *erosion* and *deposition*. Explain that students will be making a stream table to model the effects of erosion and deposition. Caution students to handle the water and sand carefully. Tell them to wipe up any spilled water immediately.

Promote Discussion When students finish, have the groups compare results. Discuss the limitations of the model—including the accuracy and size of the model. Based on what they have learned, have students consider the effects of water erosion and deposition on land use.

Scoring Rubric

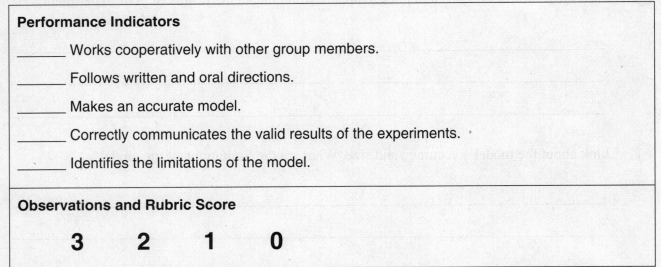

Performance Indicators
_____ Works cooperatively with other group members.
_____ Follows written and oral directions.
_____ Makes an accurate model.
_____ Correctly communicates the valid results of the experiments.
_____ Identifies the limitations of the model.

Observations and Rubric Score
3   2   1   0

What Is the Water Cycle?

1 Sofia illustrates the continuous movement of water on the surface of Earth through the water cycle.

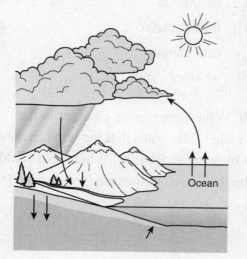

Ocean

What should she label the process of water moving down the side of a mountain?

- (A) condensation
- (B) precipitation
- (C) evaporation
- (D) runoff

2 Water on the surface of Earth constantly moves through the water cycle. Which word describes surface water that seeps into the ground?

- (A) runoff
- (B) glacier
- (C) groundwater
- (D) condensation

3 Water continuously moves above the surface of Earth through the water cycle. As water vapor rises, it cools to form water droplets. What forms when billions of these water droplets are close together?

- (A) clouds
- (B) air currents
- (C) transpiration
- (D) condensation

4 Oceans receive fresh water from precipitation and rivers. Yet the sea levels of oceans do not change very much from these actions. Why are the sea levels affected so little?

- (A) Water seeps underground beneath the oceans.
- (B) Water evaporates over the surface of the oceans.
- (C) Water flows back into rivers from the oceans.
- (D) Water is deposited back on land through ocean wave action.

5 Benny wants to explain the important role of the sun in the water cycle. What should he say the role is?

- (A) hardens soil
- (B) affects tides
- (C) provides energy
- (D) stops precipitation

Name _____ Date _____

What Are Types of Weather?

① Dominique records the following information in her science journal.

10 a.m.—temperature: 10 °C; wind speed: 5 km/hr; air pressure: 752 mb

11 a.m.—temperature: 12 °C; wind speed: 7 km/hr; air pressure: 754 mb

What is she recording changes in?

Ⓐ atmosphere   Ⓒ climate

Ⓑ evaporation   Ⓓ weather

② Wei measures the daily amount of precipitation for three days. He uses his data to construct this bar graph:

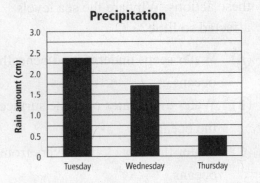

Precipitation

Based on Wei's measurements, how did the weather change over the three days?

Ⓐ The amount of rain increased.

Ⓑ The amount of rain decreased.

Ⓒ The amount of wind increased.

Ⓓ The amount of wind decreased.

③ The blue sky changes to thick gray clouds. What weather prediction is Tammy most likely to record in her science journal?

Ⓐ rainy   Ⓒ windy

Ⓑ sunny   Ⓓ very cold

④ Which of the following measures precipitation?

Ⓐ barometer

Ⓑ thermometer

Ⓒ rain gauge

Ⓓ weather vane

⑤ Dr. Peña is measuring changes in the weather. She notes that the wind in an area is blowing at 5 km/hr. Which tool could she have used to measure wind speed?

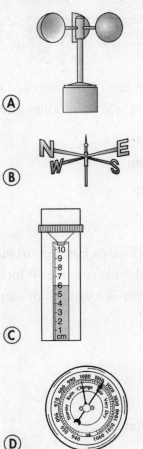

Ⓐ

Ⓑ

Ⓒ

Ⓓ

How Is Weather Predicted?

1 Use the weather maps below to predict the weather. Which weather map shows an air mass that contains warm, moist air and the possibility of rain in the forecast?

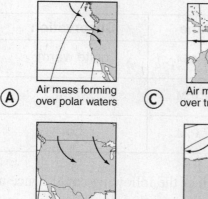

(A) Air mass forming over polar waters

(C) Air mass forming over tropical waters

(B) Air mass forming over land

(D) Air mass forming over the North Pole

2 Doppler radar uses radio waves to detect objects. It works by bouncing waves off objects to determine their location, size, and speed. For which of the following purposes do meteorologists use radar?

(A) to determine the location of storms

(B) to determine cloud type and humidity

(C) to measure average yearly precipitation amounts

(D) to determine the difference in temperature between two fronts

3 What is measured along a front?

(A) temperature and evaporation

(B) wind speed and evaporation

(C) temperature and air pressure

(D) condensation and wind direction

4 Scott views this weather map. He wants to know what the weather is going to be in Chicago. Based on the map symbols, what can Scott predict about the weather in Chicago?

(A) There is going to be a tornado.

(B) It is going to stay the same.

(C) It is going to get warmer.

(D) It is going to get colder.

5 Kanoa is reading the weather report. She uses the map key to understand the weather map. Based on the map key, Kanoa predicts that the weather in Texas will be—

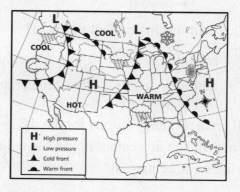

(A) cool and dry

(B) cool and cloudy

(C) warm and dry

(D) warm and wet

How Can We Observe Weather Patterns?

❶ Marissa observes that the morning sky is filled with stratus clouds. Which of the following is the best weather prediction for her to record in her science journal?

- Ⓐ cloudy all day
- Ⓑ low chance of rain
- Ⓒ heavy rain and hail
- Ⓓ strong thunderstorms

❷ Frankie was given a weather station for his birthday. The picture below shows one of the instruments on the weather station.

What will this instrument measure?

- Ⓐ rainfall
- Ⓒ air pressure
- Ⓑ humidity
- Ⓓ temperature

❸ Jill predicts heavy storms for the day. What change in weather might she record in her weather journal?

- Ⓐ Dark clouds are moving in.
- Ⓑ Barometer readings are rising.
- Ⓒ Winds appear lighter than before.
- Ⓓ Temperature has steadily increased.

❹ During a class experiment, each student recorded changes in the weather every two hours. The chart below shows the information that Bruce recorded.

Time	Observation
10 A.M.	quite warm
12 P.M.	warm
2 P.M.	hot

Which of the following could Bruce use to provide more accurate information?

- Ⓐ wind vane
- Ⓒ hygrometer
- Ⓑ barometer
- Ⓓ thermometer

❺ Carolina checks a weather map for her area. Based on the weather map, she predicts that it will be a sunny and dry day. What weather condition did she see on the map that explains her prediction?

- Ⓐ high humidity
- Ⓑ low air pressure
- Ⓒ high air pressure
- Ⓓ high precipitation

The Water Cycle and Weather

TEKS DOK Skill Builder

Use the following practice questions to help students build their comprehension skills for one TEKS at increasing depths of knowledge. The teacher notes below provide answers and strategies for diagnosing incorrect responses.

4.8B

Level 1: Recall and Reproduction

1. C; Water that falls from clouds is called precipitation. Thus stage 3 is the correct answer. **Diagnose:** To answer this question correctly, students must know the definition of *precipitation* and correctly identify the image associated with precipitation. Students who miss this question may not recall what precipitation is. Ask students to define the term. Then have them associate the definition with the cloud and rain. Discuss that 1 represents evaporation, 2 represents condensation, and 4 represents surface runoff. Have students who missed this question review the discussion of the water cycle in the Student Edition or digital lesson.

Level 2: Skills and Concepts

2. D; Sunlight heats water on Earth's surface, causing it to evaporate and form water vapor. As it rises, water vapor cools to form clouds. **Diagnose:** To answer this question correctly, students must know how the water cycle functions so they can eliminate the incorrect answers. A is incorrect because some groundwater does return to Earth's surface at places such as natural springs. B is incorrect because most water returns to Earth as precipitation. C is incorrect because the weight of water droplets and snow crystals, not the sun's heat, causes precipitation. Only D correctly states one of the processes in the water cycle. Have students who missed this question review the discussion of the water cycle in the Student Edition or digital lesson.

Level 3: Strategic Thinking

3. B; Plants and oceans are sources of water vapor. Plants release water vapor into the atmosphere through transpiration. Oceans release water vapor into the atmosphere through evaporation. **Diagnose:** Students who miss this question do not understand how water vapor enters the atmosphere. They are also failing to eliminate wrong answers. Transpiration refers to the way plants release water vapor into the atmosphere. Rainfall is the main source of groundwater. Groundwater is what is stored in the aquifer. Students who missed this question should review the discussion of the water cycle in the Student Edition or digital lesson.

The Water Cycle and Weather

Choose the letter of the best answer.

TEKS 4.8B

1 Water on and above the surface of Earth constantly moves through the water cycle. Which number represents the stage of the water cycle in which precipitation occurs?

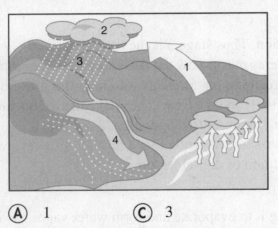

- (A) 1
- (B) 2
- (C) 3
- (D) 4

2 Which of the following is a true statement about the water cycle?

- (A) Water that seeps into the ground never returns to the water cycle.
- (B) Most of the water that evaporates from Earth's surface never returns.
- (C) Sunlight heats the water in clouds, causing the water to fall back to Earth as rain.
- (D) Sunlight heats water on Earth's surface, causing it to evaporate and form water vapor. As it rises, water vapor cools to form clouds.

3 Why are oceans and plants important to the water cycle?

- (A) Both cause transpiration.
- (B) Both are sources of water vapor.
- (C) Both are the main sources of water for the aquifer.
- (D) Both are the primary sources of groundwater.

The Water Cycle and Weather

Vocabulary and Concepts

❶ Josh watched and recorded changes in a rain puddle. The figure below shows how the puddle changes while he observes it during the day.

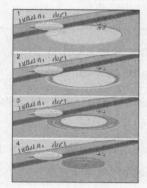

Which part of the water cycle is Josh observing?

Ⓐ   runoff   Ⓒ   precipitation

Ⓑ   evaporation   Ⓓ   condensation

TEKS 4.8B

❷ Dean writes in his weather journal: "The air feels much drier today than yesterday." What change in the weather did he record?

Ⓐ   air pressure   Ⓒ   humidity

Ⓑ   precipitation   Ⓓ   wind speed

TEKS 4.8A

❸ Which of the following processes is part of the continuous movement of water above the surface of Earth?

Ⓐ   runoff   Ⓒ   hydration

Ⓑ   recharge   Ⓓ   condensation

TEKS 4.8B

❹ Maria looks at a weather map. There is a warm front symbol pointing toward where she lives. What is the best prediction she can make about tomorrow's weather?

Ⓐ   It will be the same as today.

Ⓑ   It will be warmer and wetter than today.

Ⓒ   It will be much colder and drier than today.

Ⓓ   It will be somewhat colder and wetter than today.

TEKS 4.8A

❺ Connect weather science concepts with science careers. Which of the following describes a scientist who studies and predicts changes in the weather?

Ⓐ   archaeologist   Ⓒ   biologist

Ⓑ   meteorologist   Ⓓ   chemist

TEKS 4.3D

❻ The diagram below shows two air masses meeting.

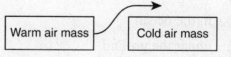

Which of the following weather changes are often recorded when a warm air mass meets a cold air mass?

Ⓐ   Wind lessens and stops.

Ⓑ   Dry air replaces moist air.

Ⓒ   Rain begins and continues.

Ⓓ   Temperatures begin to fall.

TEKS 4.8A

7 Elise illustrates the continuous movement of water above the surface of Earth through the water cycle.

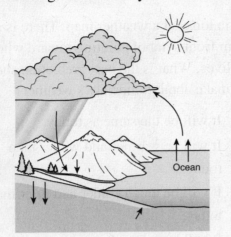

What should she label the process of water moving from the ocean to the atmosphere?

Ⓐ evaporation   Ⓒ precipitation

Ⓑ transpiration   Ⓓ condensation

TEKS 4.8B

8 A drop of water spends much more time in some stages of the water cycle than in others. Which of the following describes where a drop of water spends the shortest amount of time as it moves through the water cycle?

Ⓐ in a glacier

Ⓑ in the ocean

Ⓒ under the ground

Ⓓ in the atmosphere

TEKS 4.8B

9 A student studying the water cycle learns that for evaporation to happen, there needs to be a source of energy. What is the main source of energy that drives the water cycle?

Ⓐ the sun   Ⓒ oceans

Ⓑ wind   Ⓓ clouds

TEKS 4.8B

10 The table below shows how fresh water is distributed across Earth's surface.

Earth's freshwater sources	Fresh water (%)
Ice caps and glaciers	68.7
Groundwater	30.1
Surface water	0.3
Other	0.9

How does the table help identify the importance of water conservation?

Ⓐ It shows that ice caps and glaciers help to conserve water.

Ⓑ It shows that most fresh water is not easily available for use.

Ⓒ It shows that the most important task is conserving surface water.

Ⓓ It shows that we need to increase the other sources of fresh water.

TEKS 4.2D, 4.7C

11 Which weather symbol indicates a warm front?

TEKS 4.8A

12 Mitchell studies a weather map and sees that his area is affected by high humidity with an approaching cold front. He predicts that a thunderstorm will hit his area soon. Which observation of the weather outside would best support Mitchell's conclusion?

Ⓐ There is a light wind.

Ⓑ The temperature is 75 °F.

Ⓒ The winds are blowing from the east.

Ⓓ The clouds are mainly cumulonimbus.

TEKS 4.8A

13 Study the map key and symbols on the weather map below.

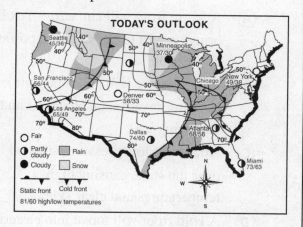

Based on the information on the map, predict what the weather will be like in Dallas.

Ⓐ cool and rainy

Ⓑ warm and cloudy

Ⓒ warm and partly cloudy

Ⓓ cold and cloudy with rain

TEKS 4.8A

14 Claire measured changes in temperature over a five-day period. She measured in Fahrenheit and then constructed the bar graph below to organize her data.

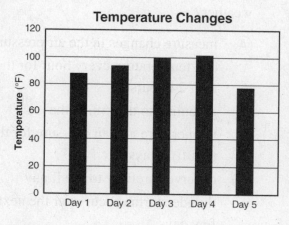

What weather event most likely occurred between the fourth and fifth day?

Ⓐ cold front and thunderstorms

Ⓑ stationary front and clear skies

Ⓒ reverse front and high humidity

Ⓓ warm front and continuous rain

TEKS 4.2C, 4.2D, 4.8A

15 Dina illustrates the continuous movement of water through the water cycle. What label does she place on line 1 to show how water moves through the water cycle above the surface of Earth?

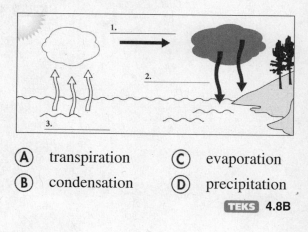

Ⓐ transpiration   Ⓒ evaporation

Ⓑ condensation   Ⓓ precipitation

TEKS 4.8B

16 A weather forecaster predicts that the weather will get colder over the next few days because a cold front is approaching. How should he verify this change in weather?

Ⓐ measure changes in the air pressure and temperature every hour for the next 24 hours

Ⓑ go online to determine the temperature and air pressure for the past five days

Ⓒ observe carefully to see if any thunderstorms occur over the next few days

Ⓓ use a barometer and thermometer to record the air pressure and temperature for five days

TEKS 4.3D, 4.8A

17 Scientists use the Celsius scale for measuring. This important contribution to science was named for Anders Celsius (1701–1744). Connect the past with the present. Which tool do weather forecasters use today that relies on the Celsius scale?

Ⓐ barometer   Ⓒ hygrometer

Ⓑ thermometer   Ⓓ anemometer

TEKS 4.3D

18 Weather maps are used to make predictions about the weather.

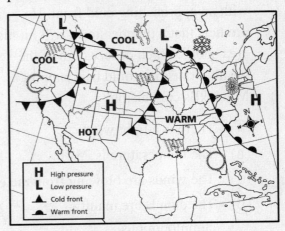

Study the map key and the symbols on the map. What is the best prediction you can make about the weather in Texas?

Ⓐ A warm front will cut across Texas, bringing rain to the southern portions of the state.

Ⓑ Low pressure will enter the state, bringing severe thunderstorms and damaging hail.

Ⓒ An area of low pressure will stall over the state, causing high temperatures and clear skies.

Ⓓ A cold front will move into eastern Texas, causing widely scattered showers and dropping temperatures.

TEKS 4.8A

Apply Inquiry and Review the Big Ideas
Write the answers to these questions.

19 Explain the role of the sun in the water cycle.

_____

_____

TEKS 4.8B

20 How are weather maps used to predict the weather?

_____

_____

TEKS 4.8A

21 Identify and describe the purpose of two tools weather forecasters use to measure changes in the weather.

_____

_____

TEKS 4.8A

22 Describe the water cycle process using the following terms: *surface runoff, groundwater, transpiration, evaporation, condensation,* and *precipitation.*

_____

_____

TEKS 4.8B

23 Analyze the data in the table below. What is the average air temperature for the week?

	M	T	W	TH	F
Air temp. (°C)	34	33	35	25	28

			.
⓪	⓪	⓪	
①	①	①	
②	②	②	
③	③	③	
④	④	④	
⑤	⑤	⑤	
⑥	⑥	⑥	
⑦	⑦	⑦	
⑧	⑧	⑧	
⑨	⑨	⑨	

TEKS 4.2D

Make a Weather Map

Materials

colored markers   pencil

Procedure

Use the information in your Student Edition to construct a map, using tools to organize, examine, and evaluate data. Complete the map below using standard symbols, or invent your own, and different colors to show the following weather conditions:

• a cold front in the Northwest

• cloudy conditions in the Southwest

• rain in the Midwest

• snow in the Northeast

• sunny conditions in the Southeast

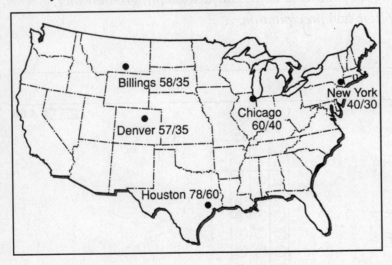

Make a Weather Map

Materials Performance Task sheet, colored markers, pencil

Time 20–30 minutes

Suggested Grouping small groups

Inquiry Skills communicate, interpret data

Preparation Hints Set up areas where small groups of students can work. You may want to provide samples of weather maps and symbols for students to review. Explain that on a weather map, the high and low air temperature in a place is sometimes shown separated by a slash as in "62/40."

Introduce the Task Ask students to reread the section about weather maps in their textbook. Point out the sections that contain information about symbols commonly used in weather maps. Ask students to discuss other symbols they have seen on weather maps. Tell students they may be creative but the symbols they use must be easily understood.

Promote Discussion When students have finished, ask one person from each group to share the group's map. Have group members explain why they chose each color and symbol and why they think their map is user-friendly.

Scoring Rubric

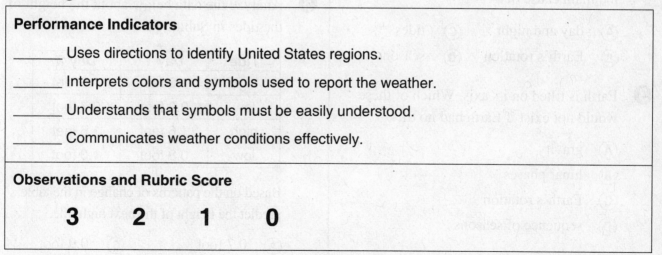

Performance Indicators

_____ Uses directions to identify United States regions.

_____ Interprets colors and symbols used to report the weather.

_____ Understands that symbols must be easily understood.

_____ Communicates weather conditions effectively.

Observations and Rubric Score

3   2   1   0

How Do the Sun, Earth, and Moon Interact?

1 Jazmin is analyzing the following data to predict patterns of change in the seasons over time.

Month	Northern Hemisphere	Southern Hemisphere
May	spring	fall
August	summer	?
November	fall	spring
January	winter	summer

What prediction can she make about August in the Southern Hemisphere?

(A) It will be fall.

(B) It will be winter.

(C) It will be spring.

(D) It will be summer.

2 The pull of the moon's gravity on Earth is the main cause of—

(A) day and night   (C) tides

(B) Earth's rotation   (D) seasons

3 Earth is tilted on its axis. Which of these would not exist if Earth had no tilt?

(A) gravity

(B) lunar phases

(C) Earth's rotation

(D) sequence of seasons

4 Analyze the data below about the tides in Galveston Channel over a two-day period.

Tide	Day 1	Day 2
high	4:29 A.M.	4:46 A.M.
low	10:02 A.M.	10:40 A.M.
high	4:17 P.M.	5:21 P.M.
low	10:24 P.M.	11:06 P.M.

Which statement correctly identifies the sequence of change in the tides?

(A) A high tide is followed by a low tide about every 6 hours.

(B) A low tide is followed by a high tide about every 12 hours.

(C) A low tide is followed by another low tide about every 9 hours.

(D) A high tide is followed by another high tide about every 10 hours.

5 Analyze the data below about the height of the tides in Sabine Pass.

Tide	Day 1	Day 2
high	1.6 feet	1.6 feet
low	0.9 foot	0.7 foot
high	1.6 feet	1.6 feet
low	0.8 foot	1.0 foot

Based on the patterns of change in the table, predict the height of the next high tide.

(A) 0.7 foot   (C) 0.9 foot

(B) 0.8 foot   (D) 1.6 feet

How Do Shadows Change?

1 Jess is collecting data on tree shadows so that she can predict patterns of change in the shadows over time. Which tool would be most helpful in collecting the data?

(A) calculator

(C) meterstick

(B) metric ruler

(D) spring scale

2 Analyze the pattern of shadows in the pictures. Which statement is true?

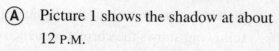

(A) Picture 1 shows the shadow at about 12 P.M.

(B) Picture 2 shows the shadow at about 12 P.M.

(C) Both pictures show the shadow at about the same time of day.

(D) Picture 1 shows the shadow in the morning and Picture 2 shows it in the afternoon.

3 Lou is collecting data to identify sequences of change in shadows. When the sun is directly overhead, how will Lou most likely describe the shadow made by his neighbor's mailbox?

(A) wide

(B) thin and long

(C) too short to see clearly

(D) as long as the mailbox is tall

4 How is the position of the sun in the sky related to the patterns found in shadows?

(A) The position of the sun has no effect on shadows.

(B) Shadows become shorter as the sun moves higher in the sky.

(C) Shadows become shorter as the sun moves lower in the sky.

(D) Shadows become longer as the sun moves higher in the sky.

5 Students set up an observational test to identify sequences of change in shadows. They measured the length of a flagpole's shadow at four different times during the school day.

9 A.M.	11 A.M.	12 P.M.	2 P.M.
6.1 m	4.2 m	3.3 m	5.1 m

Analyze the students' data. What was the sequence of change in the shadow?

(A) The length of the shadow increased throughout the day.

(B) The length of the shadow decreased throughout the day.

(C) The length of the shadow increased in the morning and decreased in the afternoon.

(D) The length of the shadow decreased until noon and then increased in the afternoon.

What Are Moon Phases?

1 The same side of the moon always faces Earth. Why is this?

(A) Half the moon faces the sun.

(B) The moon does not rotate as Earth does.

(C) The moon's rotation and orbit around Earth take the same amount of time.

(D) Earth blocks part of the sunlight that would shine on the moon's surface.

2 Dennis observes that the moon's appearance seems to change every week. Which sentence explains why?

(A) The moon moves between Earth and the sun.

(B) The moon rotates only once in about a month.

(C) The same side of the moon always faces Earth.

(D) The amount of the lighted part of the moon that faces Earth changes.

3 The observable appearance of the moon changes over time. Analyze the picture below to identify where the moon is in the sequence of changes.

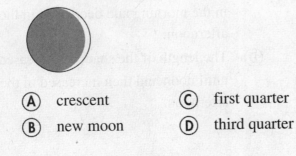

(A) crescent

(B) new moon

(C) first quarter

(D) third quarter

4 Santiago observes the night sky and draws the following picture of the moon.

He analyzes the data to predict the pattern of change in the moon. What phase does Santiago predict will happen next?

(A) full moon

(B) new moon

(C) first quarter

(D) third quarter

5 Lara collected data each night on the phases of the moon to identify the sequences of change over time. She drew pictures to show each phase. Which of the following shows the correct sequence of changes in the moon she observed?

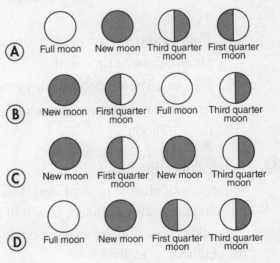

(A) Full moon   New moon   Third quarter moon   First quarter moon

(B) New moon   First quarter moon   Full moon   Third quarter moon

(C) New moon   First quarter moon   New moon   Third quarter moon

(D) Full moon   New moon   First quarter moon   Third quarter moon

How Does the Moon Move Around Earth?

❶ Earth revolves around the sun. What object does the moon revolve around as it goes through its phases?

(A) Earth

(B) its axis

(C) the sun

(D) its equator

❷ What would happen to the moon's sequences of change if the moon still revolved but Earth did not?

(A) Phases would not occur.

(B) The cycle of phases would be faster.

(C) The cycle of phases would be slower.

(D) Phases would occur the same as they do now.

❸ Hannah looks up at the moon at night and charts its appearance. She notes that the moon appears to change shape every few nights yet its features remain the same. Analyze why the moon's surface features always look the same.

(A) All features on the moon look the same.

(B) The moon's rotation distorts its features.

(C) Features on the moon's surface never change.

(D) The same side of the moon always faces Earth.

❹ Maurice collects data on changes in the appearance of the moon over a month's time. He analyzes the data and identifies that the moon goes through its sequence of phases each month. Which phase takes place when the moon is directly between Earth and the sun?

(A) full moon

(B) new moon

(C) quarter moon

(D) crescent moon

❺ Dhyana is asked to collect data on the appearance of the moon so that she can predict patterns of change over time. She observes the night sky and draws this picture of the moon.

Why would collecting this data help her predict patterns of change?

(A) It will not help her predict patterns of change.

(B) If she knows what the moon looks like, she can tell what phase it is in.

(C) If she knows the current phase of the moon, she can predict the next phase.

(D) If she knows what the moon looks like, she can predict where it is positioned between the sun and Earth.

Patterns in the Sky

TEKS DOK Skill Builder

Use the following practice questions to help students build their comprehension skills for one
TEKS at increasing depths of knowledge. The teacher notes below provide answers and
strategies for diagnosing incorrect responses.

4.8C

Level 1: Recall and Reproduction

1. D; When it is winter in the Northern Hemisphere, it is summer in the Southern Hemisphere.
    Diagnose: Students who miss this question might not recall that the seasons are opposite in the
    Northern and Southern Hemispheres. Thus if it is winter in the Northern Hemisphere, it will be
    summer in the Southern Hemisphere. Have students who missed the question review the
    discussion of seasons in the Student Edition or digital lesson.

Level 2: Skills and Concepts

2. A; Number 1 shows the tilt of the Northern Hemisphere in summer. **Diagnose:** To answer this
    question correctly, students must know that the seasons are caused by the tilt of Earth's axis and
    its orbit. They must also examine the diagram to determine at which number North America and
    Earth's axis are pointing toward the sun. Ask students what causes the seasons. Then have them
    examine the diagram to find the correct position for summer in the Northern Hemisphere.
    Students who miss this question should review the discussion of seasons in the Student Edition
    or digital lesson.

Level 3: Strategic Thinking

3. B; The water would be deepest at the dock during high tide. The highest points of high tide are at
    10 p.m. and 10 a.m. **Diagnose:** To answer this question correctly, students need to associate the
    depth of the water at the dock with high and low tide. Then they need to study the graph to find
    the times for high tide. Students who miss this question are either not making the connection
    between water depth and high tide or they are reading the graph incorrectly. Ask students how
    high tide affects water (the water comes farther onshore or gets deeper near the shoreline). Then
    ask students to explain the graph. Have them focus on the labels and the line until they
    understand that the highest points of high tide are at 10 p.m. and 10 a.m.

Patterns in the Sky

Choose the letter of the best answer.

TEKS 4.8C

1 When it is winter in the Northern Hemisphere, what season is it in the Southern Hemisphere?

Ⓐ fall

Ⓑ winter

Ⓒ spring

Ⓓ summer

2 Look at the diagram below. Which number shows the tilt of the Northern Hemisphere in the summer?

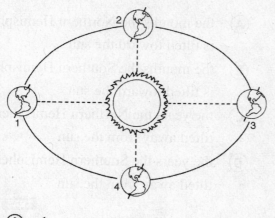

Ⓐ 1

Ⓑ 2

Ⓒ 3

Ⓓ 4

3 Look at the graph below. At what times of day would the water be the deepest at the dock?

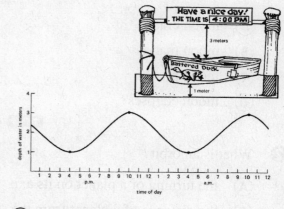

Ⓐ 4 p.m. and 4 a.m.

Ⓑ 10 p.m. and 10 a.m.

Ⓒ between 4 p.m. and 10 p.m.

Ⓓ between 10 p.m. and 10 a.m.

Patterns in the Sky

Vocabulary and Concepts

1 Identify sequences of change in the moon over time. What causes changes in the appearance of the moon's shape?

(A) moon craters

(B) moon marias

(C) moon phases

(D) moon eclipses

TEKS 4.8C

2 What is an orbit?

(A) the turning of a planet on its axis

(B) the distance of a planet from the sun

(C) the speed at which a planet moves around the sun

(D) the path one object takes around another object in space

TEKS 4.8C

3 Earth revolves around the sun while tilted on its axis. Which of these is the result of Earth's revolution while tilted?

(A) seasons

(B) shadows

(C) day and night

(D) moon phases

TEKS 4.8C

4 What are tides?

(A) changes in ocean temperatures

(B) rotations of the moon on its axis

(C) revolutions of the moon around Earth

(D) rise and fall in the water level of the ocean

TEKS 4.8C

5 What is a constellation?

(A) the rotation of Earth around an axis

(B) the system formed by the sun, Earth, and the moon

(C) a group of stars that seem to form a picture in the night sky

(D) the revolution the moon makes around Earth each month

6 Leslie wants to predict the change of seasons over time. What data should she collect to predict when it will be summer in the Southern Hemisphere?

(A) the months the Northern Hemisphere is tilted toward the sun

(B) the months the Southern Hemisphere is tilted toward the sun

(C) the years the Northern Hemisphere is tilted away from the sun

(D) the years the Southern Hemisphere is tilted away from the sun

TEKS 4.8C

7 Shane needs to collect data to identify the sequences of change in tides. What information should he collect?

(A) the height of the high tide

(B) the time each low tide occurs

(C) the time each high tide and low tide occur

(D) the time each high tide occurs and its height

TEKS 4.8C

8 Alejandro wants to identify sequences of change in shadows. Which is the best method for him to use to collect the data?

(A) use a meterstick to measure the length of an object's shadow at 10 A.M. and at 10 P.M.

(B) use a meterstick to measure the length of an object's shadow at different times throughout the day

(C) use a meterstick to measure the length of an object's shadow at 12 P.M. every day for a week

(D) use a meterstick to measure the length of an object's shadow once on a cloudy day and once on a sunny day

TEKS 4.4A, 4.8C

9 Which series identifies the sequences of change in shadows?

(A) long in the morning, shortest at noon, long toward the end of the day

(B) long in the morning, longer at noon, short toward the end of the day

(C) short in the morning, long at noon, short toward the end of the day

(D) short in the morning, longest at noon, shortest toward the end of the day

TEKS 4.8C

10 The picture below shows one of the phases of the moon.

Identify the moon phase you observe from Earth.

(A) crescent   (C) first quarter

(B) full moon   (D) third quarter

TEKS 4.8C

11 Dr. Liang needs to predict patterns of change in tides over the course of a month. She knows that the pull of the moon's gravity is the main cause of tides. Which of the following data should Dr. Liang collect so that she can predict the height of tides?

(A) the height of waves near the shore in different parts of the world

(B) the average amount of precipitation in different parts of the world

(C) the position of the sun, Earth, and the moon in relation to each other

(D) the location of storms that might affect tides in different parts of the world

TEKS 4.8C

Name _____ Date _____

12 Tiana saw the moon one night. It looked like the picture below.

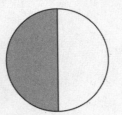

First quarter moon

One week later, she observed that the moon looked larger and noted it in her science journal. Tiana analyzed the data and concluded that—

Ⓐ the moon became larger

Ⓑ the moon became brighter

Ⓒ Earth and the moon moved closer together

Ⓓ she could see more of the side of the moon that was lit

TEKS 4.8C

13 The picture below shows the sun, the moon, and Earth.

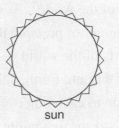

sun   Earth   moon

Which moon phase would someone on Earth observe?

Ⓐ full moon   Ⓒ last quarter

Ⓑ new moon   Ⓓ first quarter

TEKS 4.8C

14 The picture below shows the moon in several positions around Earth.

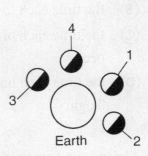

Sun

Earth

Which position would result in a person on Earth seeing a new moon?

Ⓐ 1   Ⓒ 3

Ⓑ 2   Ⓓ 4

TEKS 4.8C

15 The children in the picture below are playing in the morning. Analyze the patterns of their shadows.

Predict how the patterns will change if the children are still playing in the same place at 12 P.M.

Ⓐ Their shadows will be very short.

Ⓑ Their shadows will stay the same.

Ⓒ Their shadows will be longer and point in the other direction.

Ⓓ Their shadows will be longer and point in the same direction.

TEKS 4.8C

16 The diagram below shows Earth in different positions relative to the sun. Labels G, H, J, and K are different locations on Earth's surface.

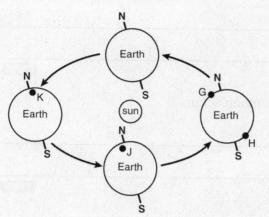

According to the diagram, which of the following correctly identifies the season for the given location?

(A) It is spring at Location G.

(B) It is winter at Location H.

(C) It is fall at Location J.

(D) It is summer at Location K.

TEKS 4.8C

17 Imagine that the moon started rotating faster. Predict the change you would observe if you were looking at it from Earth.

(A) The moon would appear dimmer.

(B) The moon would appear brighter.

(C) You could see different sides of the moon.

(D) The moon would move across the sky more quickly.

TEKS 4.8C

18 Gabrielle notices that since lunchtime her shadow seems to have grown longer than she is.

What does this tell you about the time of day?

(A) It must be near noon.

(B) It must be late in the day.

(C) It must be late in the morning.

(D) It must be early in the morning.

TEKS 4.8C

Apply Inquiry and Review the Big Ideas

Write the answers to these questions.

19 What effect does the moon have on tides?

_____

_____

TEKS 4.8C

20 What is the moon's position in space when a new moon occurs?

_____

_____

TEKS 4.8C

21 Identify four moon phases in correct sequence.

_____

_____

TEKS 4.8C

22 Draw a tree with its shadow at the two times listed below. Then explain why the shadows look different.

9 A.M.	12 P.M.

_____

_____

_____

TEKS 4.8C

23 Analyze the high tide data in the table below. Choose the number that should replace the "X" in the table. Fill in the grid with the correct number rounded to the nearest whole number.

	6 A.M.	12 P.M.	6 P.M.	12 A.M.	6 A.M.
High tide (in feet)	8.94		8.88		X

3.43	4.45	2.23	8.89	5.20	4.22	1.91

TEKS 4.8C

Chart the Seasons

Materials

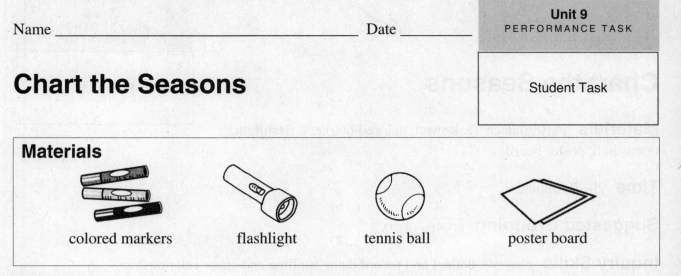

colored markers   flashlight   tennis ball   poster board

Procedure

Use the materials provided by your teacher to observe, collect data, and sequence changes in seasons. Show the sequence of seasons for the Northern Hemisphere.

❶ Use one piece of poster board to make four signs representing the four seasons. Divide another poster board into four sections and label the seasons in correct sequence.

❷ Use a marker to add the equator to the tennis ball.

❸ Use a marker to add a line representing Earth's tilted axis to the tennis ball.

❹ One person will hold the flashlight and be the "sun." Four people will hold signs indicating the seasons and stand in sequence around the "sun." One person will hold "Earth" and move around the "sun." The "sun" will rotate and illuminate Earth as Earth "revolves" around it.

❺ As "Earth" moves around the "sun," each person representing a season will illustrate the tilt of Earth and the season on the poster board.

❻ Explain why the Northern Hemisphere and Southern Hemisphere experience opposite seasons.

_____

_____

_____

_____

Chart the Seasons

Materials Performance Task sheet, colored markers, flashlight, tennis ball, poster board

Time 20–30 minutes

Suggested Grouping groups of six

Inquiry Skills observe, collect and record data, use time and space relationships

Preparation Hints Set up areas where groups of six students can work. A polystyrene foam ball can be substituted for the tennis ball.

Introduce the Task Have students reread the section about seasons in their textbook. Remind students that Earth's tilted axis does not change as it revolves around the sun. Use a group of six students to demonstrate how students will be placed for the activity. Explain that as each season is identified, the person representing that season will illustrate it on the poster board.

Promote Discussion When students have finished, ask one person from each group to share the group's season chart. Discuss why seasons change. Then use students and the season signs to demonstrate why opposite seasons take place in the Northern Hemisphere and Southern Hemisphere.

Scoring Rubric

Performance Indicators
_____ Correctly sequences seasons.
_____ Correctly illustrates each season and Earth's tilt.
_____ Correctly explains why the Northern and Southern Hemispheres experience opposite seasons.
_____ Correctly communicates why seasons change.
Observations and Rubric Score
3   **2**   **1**   **0**

How Do Organisms Obtain and Use Food?

1 Decomposers break down wastes and dead things for food. Decomposers include mushrooms and bacteria. Which of the following could provide food for a decomposer?

Ⓐ large rocks

Ⓑ fallen leaves

Ⓒ small insects

Ⓓ rays of sunlight

2 Mrs. Teller follows a vegan diet. This means she does not eat meat or any other animal products. She gets all of the nutrients she needs from plant products. Which word describes Mrs. Teller?

Ⓐ consumer   Ⓒ omnivore

Ⓑ producer   Ⓓ decomposer

3 Jamie is investigating the characteristics of consumers. Which statement is true about consumers?

Ⓐ Consumers need water to produce food.

Ⓑ Consumers produce food for other organisms.

Ⓒ Consumers are dependent on other organisms for food.

Ⓓ Consumers use energy from sunlight to produce food.

4 A student is investigating how producers need sunlight to make food. Which of the following needs sunlight to make its own food?

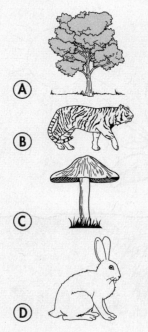

Ⓐ

Ⓑ

Ⓒ

Ⓓ

5 Hyenas, vultures, and opossums are scavengers. They get their food from eating dead things. Which statement best describes scavengers?

Ⓐ They eat producers.

Ⓑ They are producers.

Ⓒ They are consumers.

Ⓓ They eat decomposers

What Do Plants Need to Make Food?

Vera investigates what most producers need to make their own food. She makes the labeled drawing below to record her data. Use the drawing to answer Questions 1 and 2.

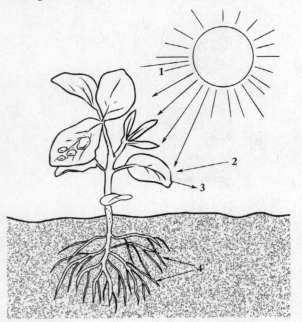

❶ Which number in the drawing shows that most producers need sunlight to make their own food?

(A) 1   (C) 3

(B) 2   (D) 4

❷ Which number in the drawing shows that most producers need carbon dioxide to make their own food?

(A) 1   (C) 3

(B) 2   (D) 4

❸ Matthew investigates what plants need to make their own food. He puts a plant on a sunny windowsill. He uses a hand lens to collect data each day for a week. On the final day, what data is he likely to have recorded?

(A) The plant wilted because producers need water to make food.

(B) The plant has three more leaves.

(C) The plant is 4 centimeters taller than on the first day.

(D) The plant wilted because it doesn't need sunlight to make food.

❹ Which three things are necessary for plants to make their own food?

(A) sugar, oxygen, sunlight

(B) water, sunlight, nitrogen

(C) carbon, sunlight, compost

(D) water, carbon dioxide, sunlight

❺ Which of the following is necessary for a tree to make food for its own growth?

(A) plenty of space to grow

(B) cloudy skies to keep the leaves moist

(C) water that works its way into the ground near the roots

(D) plenty of oxygen surrounding the leaves and bark of the tree

What Are Food Chains?

1 Look at the diagram below.

Which of the following describes the flow of energy through the food web, beginning with the sun?

Ⓐ sun, grasshopper, fish, snail, rat

Ⓑ sun, rat, snail, fish, grasshopper

Ⓒ sun, cattails, grasshopper, fish, snail

Ⓓ sun, cattails, grasshopper, frog, heron

2 In a swamp, rabbits eat marsh grass. Bobcats eat rabbits. How are the rabbits and bobcats interacting?

Ⓐ Rabbits are prey and bobcats are predators.

Ⓑ Rabbits are herbivores and bobcats are prey.

Ⓒ Rabbits are consumers and bobcats are producers.

Ⓓ Rabbits are carnivores and bobcats are herbivores.

3 In a forest, deer eat plants. Snakes eat small animals and birds. Raccoons eat mice, insects, fruits, and plants. What is the raccoon?

Ⓐ producer   Ⓒ omnivore

Ⓑ carnivore   Ⓓ herbivore

4 In a desert food chain, wild pigs called peccaries eat cacti. Then coyotes eat peccaries. In a forest food chain, deer eat plants. Then wolves eat deer. How does energy move in both of these food chains?

Ⓐ from consumers to producers

Ⓑ from producers to consumers

Ⓒ from scavengers to herbivores

Ⓓ from consumers to consumers

5 Look at the food web below.

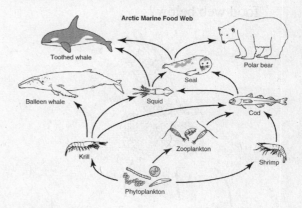

Arctic Marine Food Web

Toothed whale

Balleen whale

Seal

Polar bear

Squid

Cod

Krill

Zooplankton

Shrimp

Phytoplankton

An oil spill brings a decrease in the number of krill. Predict how this change in the ecosystem would affect the food web.

Ⓐ The number of squid would increase.

Ⓑ The amount of phytoplankton in the water would decrease.

Ⓒ Toothed whales would feed more often on seals as the number of seals increased.

Ⓓ The population of seals would decrease as a result of a decrease in the number of cod.

How Can We Model a Food Web?

1 In a food web, energy is transferred between organisms. When an organism dies, what happens to the energy stored in its body?

Ⓐ Animals use it to grow strong.

Ⓑ Fungi and bacteria use it for food.

Ⓒ Plants use it to make their own food.

Ⓓ The organism rots and its energy is lost.

2 What is the main source of energy for the food web below?

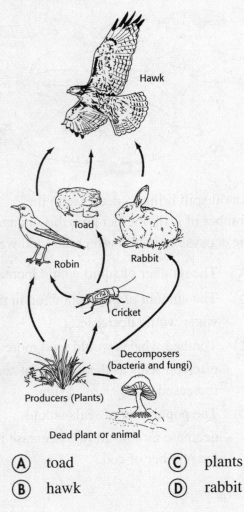

Hawk

Toad Rabbit

Robin

Cricket

Decomposers (bacteria and fungi)

Producers (Plants)

Dead plant or animal

Ⓐ toad   Ⓒ plants

Ⓑ hawk   Ⓓ rabbit

3 In Tameka's garden, caterpillars sometimes eat the vegetables. Beetles eat the caterpillars. Predict the change in the garden food web if the beetle population decreased.

Ⓐ There would be no vegetables.

Ⓑ There would be more vegetables.

Ⓒ There would be fewer vegetables.

Ⓓ There would be no difference in the vegetables.

4 The picture below shows organisms that live together in a marsh. Describe the flow of energy through one food chain in the food web.

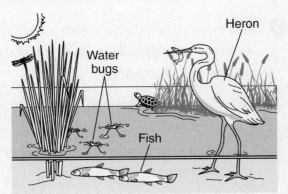

Water bugs

Heron

Fish

Ⓐ fish, water bugs, grass, heron

Ⓑ water bugs, sun, grass, fish, heron

Ⓒ heron, fish, sun, grass, water bugs

Ⓓ sun, grass, water bugs, fish, heron

5 All living things need energy. What is the main source of energy for living things?

Ⓐ sunlight   Ⓒ soil

Ⓑ plants   Ⓓ air

Organisms and Their Environments

TEKS DOK Skill Builder

Use the following practice questions to help students build their comprehension skills for one TEKS at increasing depths of knowledge. The teacher notes below provide answers and strategies for diagnosing incorrect responses.

4.9A

Level 1: Recall and Reproduction

1. A; Producers need water, carbon dioxide, and sunlight to make food. **Diagnose:** Students who miss this question might not recall that producers use water, carbon dioxide, and sunlight to make their own food. The other answer choices are consumers, not producers. Consumers cannot make their own food. Have students who missed this question review the discussion of producers and consumers in the Student Edition or digital lesson.

Level 2: Skills and Concepts

2. D; Numbers 1 and 2 are consumers, thus they cannot make their own food. **Diagnose:** To answer this question correctly, students need to understand the difference between producers and consumers so they can pick out the consumers in the diagram. Ask students to define *producers* and *consumers*. Then have them identify which numbers represent consumers. Have students who missed this question review the discussion of producers and consumers in the Student Edition or digital lesson.

Level 3: Strategic Thinking

3. B; The leaves are taking in carbon dioxide and releasing oxygen. **Diagnose:** To answer this question correctly, students need to understand how plants make their own food and associate the process with the diagram. Ask students to describe what is happening at each number in the diagram. If students cannot identify that a leaf (3) takes in sunlight (2) and carbon dioxide (4) and releases oxygen (4) as part of the process of making food, have them review the discussion in the Student Edition or digital lesson.

Organisms and Their Environments

Choose the letter of the best answer.

TEKS 4.9A

1 Which of the following need water, carbon dioxide, and sunlight to make food?

Ⓐ producers

Ⓑ consumers

Ⓒ omnivores

Ⓓ decomposers

2 Look at the diagram below.

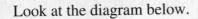

Which number represents organisms that cannot make their own food?

Ⓐ 1

Ⓑ 2

Ⓒ 3

Ⓓ 1 and 2

3 Look at the diagram below. What is being taken in and released at 4?

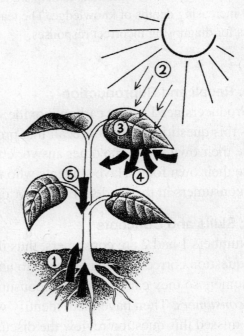

Ⓐ The leaves are taking in oxygen and releasing nitrogen.

Ⓑ The leaves are taking in carbon dioxide and releasing oxygen.

Ⓒ The leaves are taking in sunlight and releasing carbon dioxide.

Ⓓ The leaves are taking in water vapor and releasing carbon dioxide.

Organisms and Their Environments

Vocabulary and Concepts

1 A fire suddenly changes a forest's ecosystem. Predict what effect the fire might have on the forest's food web.

(A) Carnivores would suffer the most.

(B) There would be no effect on the food web.

(C) Consumers would suffer because of a lack of producers.

(D) Producers would suffer because of a lack of consumers.

TEKS 4.9B

2 People are part of food chains. What is the role of a person in a food chain?

(A) producer   (C) decomposer

(B) consumer   (D) prey

TEKS 4.9B

3 Look at the pictures below. Which needs carbon dioxide to make its own food?

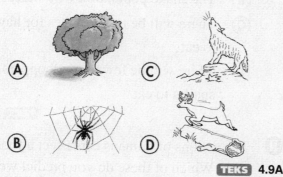

(A)   (C)

(B)   (D)

TEKS 4.9A

4 Which statement correctly describes a food web?

(A) Energy for a food web ends with the first consumer.

(B) There is less energy in a food web during the summer.

(C) The sun's energy flows from producers to consumers.

(D) Consumers store the sun's energy and pass it to producers.

TEKS 4.9B

5 Which of the following describes a science career that studies the interaction of animals and nature?

(A) chemist

(B) nutritionist

(C) industrialist

(D) environmentalist

TEKS 4.3D

6 In a swamp, archerfish live among the mangrove tree roots. In or near the water, herons feed on fish, frogs, and insects. Which term describes the archerfish and herons?

(A) omnivores   (C) herbivores

(B) producers   (D) consumers

TEKS 4.9A

Name _____ Date _____

7 The picture below shows a pond ecosystem. What is the primary source of the energy that flows through the pond's food web?

Ⓐ sun

Ⓑ water

Ⓒ plants

Ⓓ tadpoles

TEKS 4.9B

8 Ecosystems have producers, consumers, and decomposers. Why are producers important in an ecosystem?

Ⓐ They produce food for consumers.

Ⓑ They break down the remains of dead plants.

Ⓒ They produce food for other producers.

Ⓓ They consume food for other consumers.

TEKS 4.9B

9 In a forest, deer eat plants. Snakes eat small animals and birds. Raccoons eat mice, insects, fruits, and plants. What is the snake?

Ⓐ herbivore

Ⓑ carnivore

Ⓒ producer

Ⓓ decomposer

TEKS 4.9B

10 The picture below shows a food chain. One link in the food chain is missing due to a severe drought.

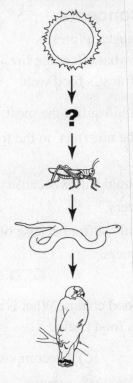

What will be the effect of the missing link on the food chain?

Ⓐ The hawk population will increase.

Ⓑ The snake population will increase.

Ⓒ There will be more snakes for hawks to eat.

Ⓓ There will be fewer grasshoppers for snakes to eat.

TEKS 4.9B

11 The actions of humans can affect a food web. Which of these do you predict would negatively affect a food web?

Ⓐ encouraging the growth of flowers

Ⓑ removing large sections of grassland

Ⓒ introducing prairie plants to a region

Ⓓ promoting native habitats in lakes and ponds

TEKS 4.9B

12 What might happen to the flow of energy in a food web during long periods of cool weather, little rain, and cloudy skies?

(A) It should increase because producers do better with little sunshine and little rain.

(B) It should increase because there will be an increase in the number of producers.

(C) It should decrease because producers depend on sunlight and water to make food.

(D) It should decrease because there will be an increase in the number of consumers.

TEKS 4.9A

13 The pictures below show some animals you might find in grassland food chains.

1

3

2

4

Which animal is the carnivore?

(A) 1   (C) 3

(B) 2   (D) 4

TEKS 4.9B

14 In a grassland food chain, grasshoppers eat grass and meerkats eat grasshoppers. What is the main role of the meerkat in this food chain?

(A) It provides energy to the grass.

(B) It obtains energy from the grass.

(C) It provides energy to grasshoppers.

(D) It obtains energy from grasshoppers.

TEKS 4.9B

15 Food chains have three types of consumers. Which statement describes a herbivore?

(A) eats only plants

(B) eats only animals

(C) makes its own food

(D) eats plants and animals

TEKS 4.9B

16 Which gas do most producers need to make their own food?

(A) helium   (C) oxygen

(B) carbon dioxide (D) methane

TEKS 4.9A

17 The diagram below shows a food web. Which shows one food chain with the hawk?

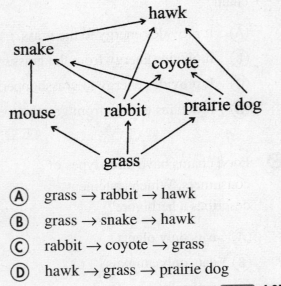

(A) grass → rabbit → hawk

(B) grass → snake → hawk

(C) rabbit → coyote → grass

(D) hawk → grass → prairie dog

TEKS 4.9B

18 The picture below shows organisms in an ecosystem.

What do the organisms shown in the picture have in common?

(A) They are all dependent upon other organisms for food.

(B) They all need sunlight, water, and carbon dioxide to make food.

(C) They are all herbivores.

(D) They all need sunlight, water, and oxygen to make food.

TEKS 4.9A

Apply Inquiry and Review the Big Ideas
Write the answers to these questions.

19 Explain the importance of producers in a food chain.

_____

_____

TEKS 4.9A, 4.9B

20 What three things do producers need to make their own food?

_____

_____

TEKS 4.9A

21 How does energy flow in a food web?

_____

_____

TEKS 4.9B

22 There is a flood in a forest ecosystem. Remove an organism from this food chain and predict how the change will affect the flow of energy within the food chain.

_____

_____

TEKS 4.9B

23 How many food chains in the food web below include the fox or the snake?

TEKS 4.9B

Student Task

Food Chain

Materials

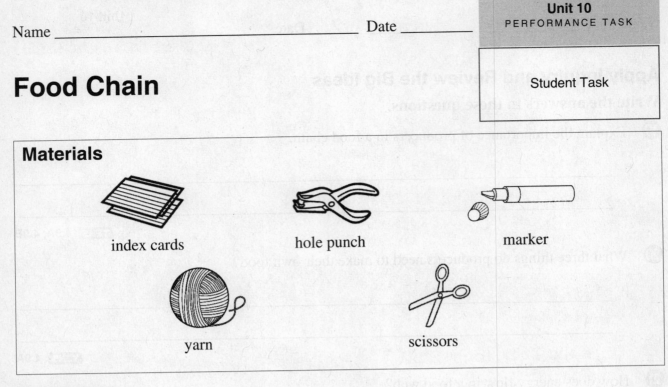

index cards

hole punch

marker

yarn

scissors

Procedure

grass

grasshopper

owl

shrew

❶ Read the list of organisms. These organisms are part of a food chain.

❷ Write the name of each organism on an index card.

❸ Punch a hole on either end of each card.

❹ Arrange the cards on your desk so that producers are at the bottom, followed by consumers that eat producers, with consumers that eat other consumers at the top.

❺ Use yarn to connect the cards to make a food chain. Compare your food chain with those of others in the class.

❻ Suppose a drought caused the grass to turn brown and wither away. Write a paragraph to describe how this change in the ecosystem would affect your food chain.

Food Chain

Materials Performance Task sheet, index cards, hole punch, markers, yarn, scissors

Time 30 minutes

Suggested Grouping groups of two to four

Inquiry Skills make a model, observe

Preparation Hints Cut a length of yarn for each group. If possible, have an illustration of each organism to show the class.

Introduce the Task Ask students to describe a food chain. Tell them they are going to make a model to show how energy flows through a food chain. Model how to mark cards, punch holes, and tie yarn.

Promote Discussion Ask students how they chose the order in which to place the cards to form one chain. Ask students to hypothesize about the effect of adding or removing any of the consumers from the chain. Have them describe the impact of changes in the ecosystem on the food chain.

Scoring Rubric

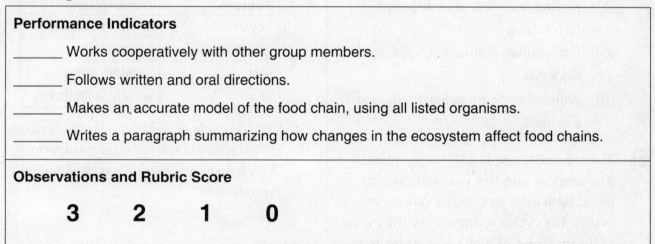

Performance Indicators

_____ Works cooperatively with other group members.

_____ Follows written and oral directions.

_____ Makes an accurate model of the food chain, using all listed organisms.

_____ Writes a paragraph summarizing how changes in the ecosystem affect food chains.

Observations and Rubric Score

3   2   1   0

How Do Plants Reproduce?

1 An empress tree is a flowering plant. This tree's flowers have blue and violet markings. What is the main role of the colored markings on the flowers?

(A) to attract insects to carry pollen

(B) to protect the plant from the sun

(C) to produce pollen for reproduction

(D) to disperse seeds to other parts of the local environment

2 The cedar tree is a nonflowering plant. The peach tree is a flowering plant. Kellie explores the life cycles of both trees and discovers they are similar. What did she find was the order of events in the life cycles of both plants?

(A) seed, pollination, seed dispersal, fertilization

(B) pollination, seed, seed dispersal, fertilization

(C) fertilization, pollination, seed, seed dispersal

(D) pollination, fertilization, seed, seed dispersal

3 The red maple tree is a flowering plant. The longleaf pine tree is a nonflowering plant. Both trees go through various stages in their life cycles. Compare the life cycles of the two trees. Which stage occurs in the lives of both trees?

(A) making fruits

(B) making cones

(C) making seeds

(D) making flowers

4 Millions of honeybees have recently vanished from their hives throughout the country. No one is sure why the bees have disappeared. However, many people are concerned. Why are people concerned about what is happening to the honeybees?

(A) Bees help with seed dispersal.

(B) Bees pollinate many flowering plants.

(C) Bees help protect seeds in nonflowering plants.

(D) Bees protect seeds until they start to germinate into seedlings.

5 Cory constructs the chart below to organize data. The chart lists some features of the greenbrier vine.

Greenbrier Vine

Feature	Description
flower	small, green-white
growth pattern	tall, twining
leaf	pointed, shiny
stem	woody, with thorns

The life cycle of a greenbrier vine includes reproduction involving eggs and sperm. Which feature of the plant is used for reproduction?

(A) leaf

(B) stem

(C) flower

(D) growth pattern

How Can We Explore a Plant's Life Cycle?

❶ Nathan wants to compare the life cycles of lima bean plants and radish plants. He plants both types of seeds in the same kind of soil. He keeps them at equal temperatures and gives them the same amount of water and light. He records how long it takes each plant to sprout. What is Nathan comparing?

- Ⓐ pollination
- Ⓑ fertilization
- Ⓒ germination
- Ⓓ seed dispersal

❷ Students are testing conditions for germinating bean seeds. Which is the best way for them to study how the amount of water affects the germination of the bean seeds?

- Ⓐ give the seeds no water and wait to see if any of the seeds will germinate
- Ⓑ give the seeds large amounts of water and watch to see if any of them will germinate
- Ⓒ give the seeds different amounts of water and record when each seed germinates
- Ⓓ give the seeds the same amount of water and watch to see which one germinates first

❸ Mario plants four bean seeds. He waters the first seed twice a day, the second seed once a day, the third seed every other day, and the fourth seed not at all. What is the tested variable in this investigation?

- Ⓐ the kind of seed
- Ⓑ the amount of water
- Ⓒ the germination rate
- Ⓓ the time of day the seed is watered

❹ Imani is comparing the effect of fertilizers on the growth of different plants. Which of the following does she need to carry out a controlled experiment?

- Ⓐ a plant that gets no fertilizer
- Ⓑ seeds of different types of plants
- Ⓒ plants that get different amounts of water
- Ⓓ a plant that is fertilized halfway through the experiment

❺ Yessica planted two radish seeds in the same kind of soil. She kept them at equal temperatures and gave them the same amount of water, but exposed them to different amounts of sunlight. What is Yessica trying to demonstrate?

- Ⓐ Soil affects plant growth rate.
- Ⓑ Plants will grow when watered.
- Ⓒ Temperature affects plant growth.
- Ⓓ Sunlight affects plant growth rate.

How Do Animals Reproduce?

❶ Erik is exploring animal life cycles. He wants to research how some animals go through metamorphosis. Which would be an example of an animal that goes through metamorphosis?

(A) coyote

(B) sea turtle

(C) nurse shark

(D) grasshopper

❷ Aaron finds a quail's nest while on a hike. He notices that a mother quail has eggs in the nest. What is likely to happen next in the life cycle of the quail eggs?

(A) flying

(B) growing

(C) hatching

(D) reproducing

❸ A mouse and her pups are in a burrow. The pups are small and still getting milk from their mother. What stage in the life cycle of the pups is this?

(A) birth

(B) growth

(C) maturity

(D) reproduction

❹ Dimitri sees an egg on the ground near the nature trail.

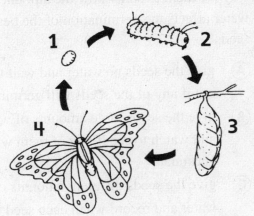

Which type of animal could be the parent of this offspring?

(A) robin

(B) skunk

(C) coyote

(D) squirrel

❺ Lumi is asked to observe and illustrate the life cycle of a butterfly. She records her data by making the drawing shown below.

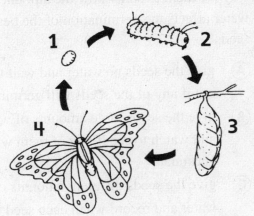

What should she label Stage 3?

(A) egg

(B) pupa

(C) larva

(D) butterfly

How Are Living Things Adapted to Their Environments?

❶ Which adaptation of this mountain lion enables it to survive in its environment by catching the deer?

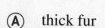

- Ⓐ thick fur
- Ⓑ long tail
- Ⓒ small ears
- Ⓓ sharp teeth

❷ Adaptations enable animals to survive in their environment. In what environment would an animal with thick white fur and a thick layer of fat most likely live?

- Ⓐ in a stream
- Ⓑ in a desert
- Ⓒ in a grassland
- Ⓓ in a polar region

❸ The animal shown below has webbed feet and a paddle-like tail. Where does this animal most likely live?

- Ⓐ in a tree
- Ⓑ in a desert
- Ⓒ near a stream
- Ⓓ in a polar region

❹ Which adaptation would you expect to find in a bird that swims?

- Ⓐ feet with feathers
- Ⓑ feet with webbing
- Ⓒ feet with large hooked claws
- Ⓓ feet with curling toes and tiny claws

❺ Which adaptation would you expect in animals that live in caves?

- Ⓐ good hearing
- Ⓑ good eyesight
- Ⓒ poor sense of smell
- Ⓓ brightly colored fur

Why Do Bird Beaks Differ?

1 A scientist is studying an extinct bird. He wants to learn more about how it was adapted to its environment. Which feature of the bird would be the best thing for him to study to discover what the bird ate?

- (A) tail
- (B) feet
- (C) beak
- (D) wings

2 Shirley is studying the birds in her neighborhood to explore adaptations. What does the bird shown below most likely eat?

- (A) mice
- (B) seeds
- (C) insects in wood
- (D) fish in shallow water

3 Joshua is comparing bird beaks to explore how adaptations enable organisms to survive in their environment. He knows that the main sources of food for birds that live in grasslands are seeds, mice, and burrowing insects. Which beak should Joshua label as least useful in grasslands?

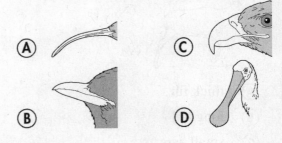

- (A)
- (C)
- (B)
- (D)

4 Which bird is most likely to eat mice and snakes?

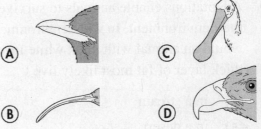

- (A)
- (C)
- (B)
- (D)

5 Tam is investigating birds in a wetland. She notices that many of the birds have similar beaks with the same kind of shape. Which statement is the most likely explanation for the similar beaks?

- (A) All birds have similar beaks.
- (B) The birds all belong to the same species.
- (C) The birds build the same types of shelters.
- (D) The birds have beaks suited to the food available.

What Are Heredity, Instincts, and Learned Behaviors?

❶ A student knows that some likenesses between parents and offspring are inherited, passed from generation to generation. Which of the following is an example of an inherited likeness in humans?

(A) eye color

(B) length of hair

(C) ability to read

(D) type of language spoken

❷ Some likenesses between parents and offspring are learned. Which of the following is a learned behavior in dogs?

(A) eating

(B) running

(C) barking

(D) shaking hands

❸ One kind of moth lives on the bark of trees. In areas where the trees and moths are located near factories, their color is dark. Where there are no factories, the same kinds of moths and trees are light colored. What is the most likely cause for this difference in color?

(A) diet

(B) instinct

(C) environment

(D) learned behavior

❹ Canada geese travel north when the weather gets warm in the spring. Then they travel south when it gets cold in late fall. Suppose that the spring temperature stayed cold two weeks longer than usual. How would that change the behavior of the geese?

(A) They would not travel north at all.

(B) They would travel north at the usual time.

(C) They would travel north about two weeks later.

(D) They would travel north about two weeks earlier.

❺ Hurricanes damage trees. If a pine tree loses half of its branches, what will its offspring look like?

(A) They will have no branches.

(B) They will have the normal number of branches.

(C) They will have twice as many branches.

(D) They will have half the normal number of branches.

Plants and Animals

TEKS DOK Skill Builder

Use the following practice questions to help students build their comprehension skills for one TEKS at increasing depths of knowledge. The teacher notes below provide answers and strategies for diagnosing incorrect responses.

4.10C

Level 1: Recall and Reproduction

1. B; The correct order is pollination, fertilization, seed, seed dispersal. **Diagnose:** To answer this question correctly, students need to understand the steps in plant reproduction. Ask students what has to happen before a plant can produce a seed (pollination and fertilization). Once students understand that pollination comes before fertilization and both are required to produce a seed, they should be able to eliminate the incorrect answers. Have students who missed this question review the discussion of plant reproduction in the Student Edition or digital lesson.

Level 2: Skills and Concepts

2. C; Stage 2 is the larva. **Diagnose:** To answer this question correctly, students need to understand the stages in the life cycle of a butterfly. They also need to be able to identify the stages visually. If students select B, they may be confusing the larva stage with the pupa stage. Ask students to define each stage. Explain that the larva stage comes before the pupa stage. To help students make the distinction, remind them that the larva is also called a caterpillar. Have students who missed the question review the discussion of the life cycle of a butterfly in the Student Edition or digital lesson.

Level 3: Strategic Thinking

3. B; Picture 2 shows germination. **Diagnose:** To answer this question correctly, students need to recall the definition of *germination* and be able to associate it with a picture of that stage of development. Students who miss this question either do not know the definition or cannot translate the definition into a visual representation. Have students who missed the question review the discussion of germination in the Student Edition or digital lesson.

Plants and Animals

Choose the letter of the best answer.

TEKS 4.10C

❶ What is the order of events in the life cycle of a plant?

  Ⓐ fertilization, pollination, seed, seed dispersal

  Ⓑ pollination, fertilization, seed, seed dispersal

  Ⓒ seed, pollination, seed dispersal, fertilization

  Ⓓ pollination, seed, seed dispersal, fertilization

❷ Max draws the life cycle of a butterfly.

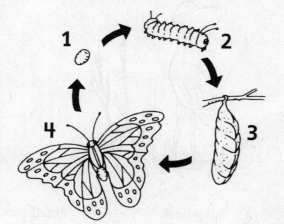

What should he label stage 2?

  Ⓐ adult

  Ⓑ pupa

  Ⓒ larva

  Ⓓ egg

❸ Look at the pictures below.

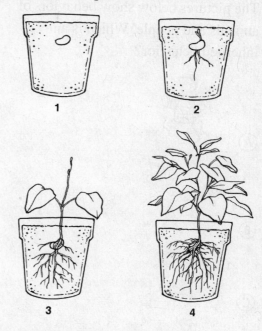

Which picture shows germination?

  Ⓐ 1

  Ⓑ 2

  Ⓒ 3

  Ⓓ 4

Plants and Animals

Vocabulary and Concepts

1 The pictures below show behaviors of animals and people. Which is an inherited behavior?

(A)

(B)

(C)

(D)

TEKS 4.10B

2 An arctic hare is brown in the summer and white in the winter. What is most likely the cause of this change?

(A) learned behavior

(B) instinctive behavior

(C) effect of environment

(D) beginning of hibernation

TEKS 4.10A

3 A female nine-banded armadillo usually has four pups at a time. Which word describes this part of the life cycle?

(A) death   (C) maturity

(B) growth   (D) reproduction

TEKS 4.10C

4 What adaptation does the deer have for escaping from the mountain lion?

(A) thick fur   (C) small ears

(B) strong legs   (D) short tail

TEKS 4.10A

5 What adaptation does the heron below have for surviving in its environment?

(A) long beak   (C) small ears

(B) short legs   (D) short beak

TEKS 4.10A

6 Mary plants a tomato seed in a wooden box with good soil. She gives it plenty of water. What will happen next in the plant's life cycle?

(A) It will flower.

(B) It will germinate.

(C) It will grow leaves.

(D) It will grow many roots.

TEKS 4.10C

7 The picture below shows a bear fishing for food.

Where does the bear learn this behavior?

Ⓐ on its own

Ⓑ from instincts

Ⓒ from its mother

Ⓓ from other bear cubs

TEKS 4.10B

8 You want to study how instincts and learning affect animals. Which of the following science careers might you choose?

Ⓐ chemist

Ⓑ environmentalist

Ⓒ horticulturalist

Ⓓ animal behaviorist

TEKS 4.3D

9 Thomas looks a lot like other members of his family. Which is a trait that he probably did not inherit from his parents?

Ⓐ size of his feet

Ⓑ shape of his ears

Ⓒ color of his eyes

Ⓓ length of his hair

TEKS 4.10B

10 The magnolia tree is a flowering plant. The pine tree is a nonflowering plant. Both trees have similar life cycles. What is the order of events in the life cycles of both plants?

Ⓐ fertilization, pollination, seed, seed dispersal

Ⓑ pollination, fertilization, seed, seed dispersal

Ⓒ seed, pollination, seed dispersal, fertilization

Ⓓ pollination, seed, seed dispersal, fertilization

TEKS 4.10C

11 The illustration below shows part of the life cycle of a nonflowering tree.

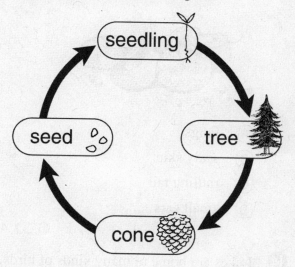

The life cycle of a nonflowering tree includes maturity. Which stage of the life cycle shows maturity?

Ⓐ tree

Ⓑ cone

Ⓒ seed

Ⓓ seedling

TEKS 4.10C

12 Ginger was doing an investigation that included the following procedure.

> Remove the stamen. Lightly wipe the tip of the stamen against the black paper. Some of the powdery pollen should stick to the paper.

What was she studying?

(A) growth of a seedling

(B) germination of a seed

(C) methods of seed dispersal

(D) reproduction in flowering plants

TEKS 4.10C

13 Which adaptation allows this animal to survive in a desert?

(A) fangs

(B) scaly skin

(C) rattling tail

(D) small ears

TEKS 4.10A

14 Lakes are home to many kinds of birds. Which feet show an adaptation inherited by a bird that swims in water to find food?

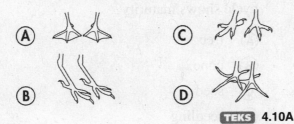

TEKS 4.10A

15 Jackson is illustrating the life cycles of different organisms. He draws the picture of a frog life cycle below.

How should he reorder the illustration so that the life cycle is in the correct order?

(A) eggs, adult, tadpole with legs, tadpole

(B) eggs, tadpole, tadpole with legs, adult

(C) adult, tadpole, tadpole with legs, eggs

(D) adult, eggs, tadpole with legs, tadpole

TEKS 4.10C

16 The picture below shows flowers with an unusual shape.

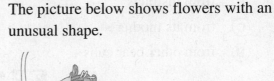

Which beak shape would best allow a bird to reach the nectar inside the flowers?

(A) long and thick

(B) short and thin

(C) long and thin

(D) short and thick

TEKS 4.10A

17 A stilt is a bird found in wetlands. It wades in shallow water and has a slender, sharp beak. What does the stilt most likely eat?

(A) seeds and nuts

(B) nectar and sap

(C) frogs and large fish

(D) insects and crustaceans

TEKS 4.10A

18 A safflower is a plant with a small seed. The seed has a thick shell. Birds need to crack open the shell to eat the seed. Which type of beak would be best suited to eating safflower seeds?

(A) short and sharp

(B) short and strong

(C) long and slender

(D) long and pointed

TEKS 4.10A

Apply Inquiry and Review the Big Ideas

Write the answers to these questions.

19 Organisms are adapted to their environments. Give an example of one physical adaptation and one behavioral adaptation and tell how each helps the organism survive. Your response should include a plant example and an animal example.

_____

_____

TEKS 4.10A

20 Seeds may remain dormant, or inactive, for days, weeks, or months after they reach the ground. This means that they do not start to germinate immediately. What is one reason that seeds may remain dormant?

_____

_____

TEKS 4.10C

21 Destiny is implementing an investigation about likenesses between parents and offspring. She observes a mother cat bathing its kittens. Over time the kittens begin to bathe themselves. What can Destiny infer about the type of likeness the cats have displayed?

_____

_____

TEKS 4.10A, 4.10B

22 Plants and animals have adaptations suitable to the environments in which they live. Compare desert hares with arctic hares. Explain two ways the hares differ in inherited adaptations. How do these adaptations help the hares survive in their environments?

_____

_____

TEKS 4.10B

23 The southern pine beetle damages pine trees all over the southern United States. The female beetle finds a tree, digs holes, and lays her eggs deep inside the trunk. An egg hatches, and the larva eats wood inside the tree. Then it crawls to the wood just under the bark, where it becomes a pupa. Once the pupa turns into a beetle, it crawls out of the tree and flies away.

How many stages of the southern pine beetle's life cycle are spent entirely in a tree?

TEKS 4.10C

Chart Inheritance

Materials

colored markers

chart paper

Procedure

Each group will make a chart of characteristics to show how likenesses between parents and offspring are inherited.

1 Use a large sheet of paper to construct a chart on inherited likenesses. Leave space in your chart for drawing pictures.

Inherited Likeness	Student _____	Student _____	Student _____

2 As a group, agree on five likenesses that are inherited. List those in the left column.

3 Each student will complete his or her column of likenesses. For example, if hair color is listed as an inherited likeness, then each student should draw and color his or her hair on the chart.

4 Share your chart with the rest of the class.

5 Think about likenesses that are not inherited but are learned, such as enjoying the same sport. What likeness do you share with one of your parents that is learned?

_____

_____

Chart Inheritance

Materials Performance Task sheet, colored markers, chart paper

Time 20–30 minutes

Suggested Grouping groups of three

Inquiry Skills collect data, analyze data, observe

Preparation Hints Set up areas where groups of three students can comfortably work with large chart paper.

Introduce the Task Review inherited and learned likenesses. Ask student volunteers to share likenesses they have with a parent, such as hair or eye color. Discuss the different likenesses that are inherited. Ask student volunteers to share things that they and a parent enjoy, such as similar sports, movies, or colors. Ask students: What is the difference between learned and inherited likenesses?

Promote Discussion When students have finished, have each group share their chart. Talk about the diversity of inherited likenesses among the students. Highlight that, though everyone inherits likenesses from his or her parents, everyone has a unique set of characteristics.

Scoring Rubric

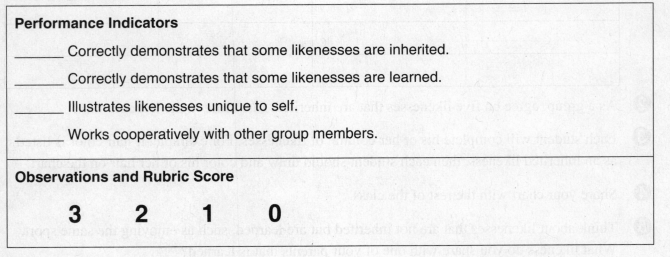

Performance Indicators
_____ Correctly demonstrates that some likenesses are inherited.
_____ Correctly demonstrates that some likenesses are learned.
_____ Illustrates likenesses unique to self.
_____ Works cooperatively with other group members.

Observations and Rubric Score

3   2   1   0

1 Alicia knows that magnetism is the property of some matter. She contrasted the strengths of four magnets. Which of her four magnets had the weakest magnetic attraction?

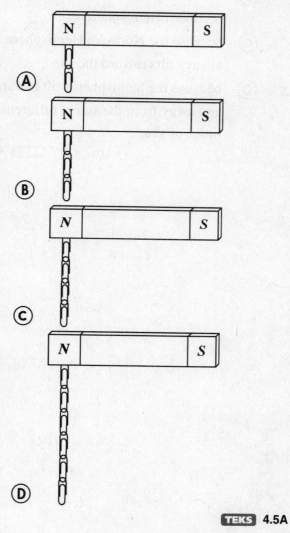

TEKS 4.5A

2 Tomás is implementing a descriptive investigation on how clouds can help forecast weather. He knows that he needs a well-defined question to guide his investigation. Given his research topic, which of the following well-defined questions would be best?

(A) How do clouds form?

(B) How can we identify different types of clouds?

(C) Why are some clouds white, while other clouds are gray?

(D) What weather conditions are associated with each type of cloud?

TEKS 4.2A

3 Natalia fills a graduated cylinder with 50 mL of water. She places a small rock inside the cylinder, as shown in the picture below.

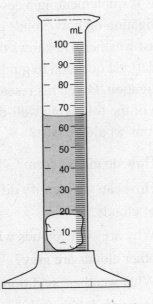

What is the volume of the rock placed inside the graduated cylinder?

Ⓐ 15 mL

Ⓑ 50 mL

Ⓒ 65 mL

Ⓓ 100 mL

TEKS 4.4A, 4.5A

4 Seasons are reversed in the Northern and Southern Hemispheres. Why do the Northern and Southern Hemispheres never experience the same season at the same time?

Ⓐ because seasons are longer in the Northern Hemisphere

Ⓑ because seasons are shorter in the Southern Hemisphere

Ⓒ because the Northern Hemisphere always tilts toward the sun

Ⓓ because the hemispheres tilt toward and away from the sun at different times of year

TEKS 4.8C

5 The scientist Galileo built the first thermometer. It was called a thermoscope.

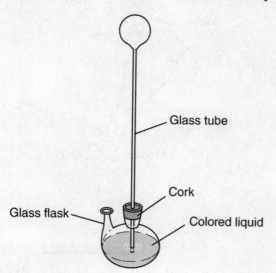

Glass tube

Cork

Glass flask

Colored liquid

Galileo would place his hands on the glass flask. The colored liquid would rise in the tube. The reason that the colored liquid rose in the glass tube is connected to which of the following concepts in science?

Ⓐ The temperature of the colored liquid dropped.

Ⓑ Galileo's hands were colder than the glass flask.

Ⓒ Heat flowed from Galileo's hands to the colored liquid.

Ⓓ Galileo put pressure on the flask and squeezed the liquid up.

TEKS 4.3D

6 Ms. Hawkins tells her class that animals are adapted to their environments. She then asks the class to analyze this scientific explanation by using logical reasoning to determine where an animal with big ears and a thin coat would live. Which environment is the logical choice?

Ⓐ desert

Ⓑ stream

Ⓒ polar region

Ⓓ underground

TEKS 4.3A, 4.10A

7 An animal's life cycle includes the stages of birth, growth, maturity, reproduction, and death. Which of the following is an example of maturity?

Ⓐ A hognose snake hatches from an egg.

Ⓑ A bald eagle grows to its full adult size.

Ⓒ An alligator lays a clutch of eggs near the banks of a swamp.

Ⓓ A white-tailed deer's heart stops beating after many years.

TEKS 4.10C

8 Which type of consumer is the hawk?

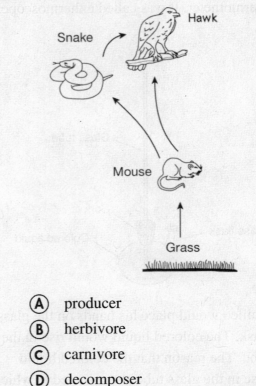

Ⓐ producer

Ⓑ herbivore

Ⓒ carnivore

Ⓓ decomposer

TEKS 4.9A

Name _____ Date _____

9 How does the shape of the moon change during the weeks after a full moon?

    (A) The lighted part of the moon seems to get bigger.

    (B) The lighted part of the moon seems to get smaller.

    (C) There is no change for two weeks after a new moon.

    (D) The lighted part of the moon disappears for several days.

TEKS 4.8C

10 Max knows that cooling can cause changes in matter. He places a tray of ice water on the picnic table in his backyard. What change does he predict will happen to the outside of the glasses when the warm air touches the cold glasses?

    (A) The air will cool and keep the outside of the glasses dry.

    (B) The air will warm and keep the outside of the glasses dry.

    (C) The air will warm and form condensation on the outside of the glasses.

    (D) The air will cool and form condensation on the outside of the glasses.

TEKS 4.5B

11 Raoul is observing the growth of seedlings. He puts a bean seed, a pumpkin seed, and a sunflower seed on a piece of wet paper towel. He places the towel inside a plastic bag and seals it. He puts the bag in a warm place and records what happens. The chart below shows his observations.

Seed Germination Chart

Day	Bean seed	Pumpkin seed	Sunflower seed
1			
2			
3	root appears		
4			
5		root appears	
6	stem appears		
7	leaves unfold		
8			root appears
9		stem appears	
10		leaves unfold	

Which conclusion could Raoul draw from these observations?

Ⓐ The sunflower seed was dead.

Ⓑ Roots emerge before stems or leaves.

Ⓒ Seeds need light and warmth to germinate.

Ⓓ Pumpkin seeds germinate more quickly than bean seeds.

TEKS 4.10C

12 Laura and Cho have designed and made two model cars, one green and one yellow. They release both cars at the top of a ramp and measure how far each car travels from the bottom of the ramp until stopping. The table shows their results.

Car	Distance traveled from bottom of ramp
Green car	3.3 meters
Yellow car	2.8 meters

What is the next step that Laura and Cho should take to increase the reliability of their results?

Ⓐ redesign the yellow car

Ⓑ communicate their results

Ⓒ test the cars two more times

Ⓓ conclude that the green car goes farther

TEKS 4.2E

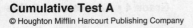

⑬ Emilio is building a model of a thermometer for his science fair project. The picture below shows what he has built so far.

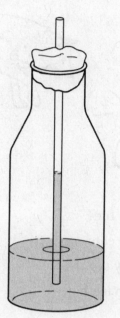

What should Emilio do to show that his model works like a real thermometer?

Ⓐ add more liquid to the bottle

Ⓑ use a larger straw inside the bottle

Ⓒ place numbers along the length of the bottle

Ⓓ put the model thermometer in different temperatures

TEKS 4.3C

⑭ The life cycles of all seed plants involve certain steps. One of these steps is illustrated below.

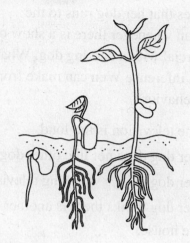

Which step occurs after the step shown above?

Ⓐ death

Ⓑ maturity

Ⓒ germination

Ⓓ reproduction

TEKS 4.10C

15 Wen is implementing a descriptive investigation on the behavior of animals. She is observing the behavior of her dog. She notes that her dog runs to the television whenever there is a show or a commercial with a barking dog. What is the best inference Wen can make from her dog's behavior?

(A) The television is too loud.

(B) Her dog does not like other dogs.

(C) Her dog enjoys watching television.

(D) Her dog thinks there is another dog in the house.

TEKS 4.2A

16 Which adaptation will help the rabbit detect the wolf so that it can escape?

(A) thick fur

(B) large ears

(C) fluffy tail

(D) sharp teeth

TEKS 4.10A

17 Benny drops a ball off a bridge. The ball drops straight down, as shown in the diagram.

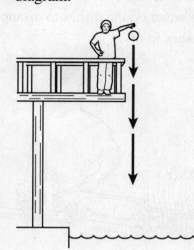

What happens to the ball as it falls?

(A) Its speed and acceleration stay the same.

(B) Its speed increases, but its acceleration decreases.

(C) Its speed decreases, but its acceleration increases.

(D) Its speed increases, but its acceleration stays the same.

TEKS 4.6D

18 Maria knows that it is important to conserve natural resources. Which of the following is an example of an informed choice her family can make to use and conserve natural resources?

(A) water the grass every day

(B) use paper towels to dry the dishes

(C) drive a car that gets good gas mileage

(D) keep the air conditioner set to a low temperature in the summer

TEKS 4.1B

19 Joy builds an electric circuit out of several pieces of wire, a light bulb, and a battery. Now she wants to add a switch to create a closed circuit. Which of the following would be best to use for a switch?

(A) cotton string

(B) plastic spoon

(C) wooden stick

(D) metal paper clip

TEKS 4.6C

20 Tiko is washing the dishes. He puts the clean, wet dishes on the drying rack. Tiko knows that over time, the water cycle causes the water on the dishes to disappear and the dishes to dry.

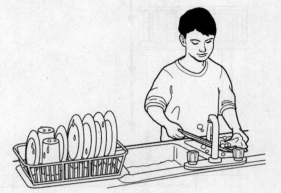

What causes the water on the clean dishes to disappear?

(A) The water melts.

(B) The water condenses.

(C) The water evaporates.

(D) The water is absorbed.

TEKS 4.8B

21 Observe the glacier below.

glacier

As a glacier moves downhill, it breaks apart rocks and other material. This slow change to Earth's surface is caused by—

Ⓐ erosion from ice

Ⓑ polishing from ice

Ⓒ deposition from ice

Ⓓ weathering from ice

TEKS 4.7B

22 Doug is conducting an experiment about the effect of force on an object by rolling tennis balls across the floor. What does he need to know in order to determine the velocity of a tennis ball?

Ⓐ speed and direction

Ⓑ time and distance

Ⓒ force and motion

Ⓓ mass and size

TEKS 4.6D

23 The ability to hold water is one of the properties of soils. Some soils retain water better than others. A student is examining different soils. Which soil has the greatest capacity to retain water?

(A) sandy soil

(B) loamy soil

(C) clay-rich soil

(D) humus-rich soil

TEKS 4.7A

24 Eva is observing and recording the weather near her home. She sees thin, wispy white clouds high in the sky. Which type of weather can she predict?

(A) cool and clear

(B) hot and stormy

(C) warm and rainy

(D) cold and snowy

TEKS 4.8A

Name _____ Date _____

25 Water on and above the surface of Earth constantly moves through the water cycle. Which number illustrates the stage of the water cycle in which condensation occurs?

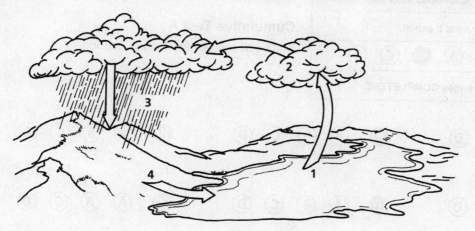

TEKS 4.8B

Name _____ Date _____

PLEASE NOTE

- Use only a no. 2 pencil.
- Example: Ⓐ ● Ⓒ Ⓓ
- Erase changes COMPLETELY.

Cumulative Test A

Mark one answer for each question.

❶ Ⓐ Ⓑ Ⓒ Ⓓ   ❿ Ⓐ Ⓑ Ⓒ Ⓓ   ⓳ Ⓐ Ⓑ Ⓒ Ⓓ

❷ Ⓐ Ⓑ Ⓒ Ⓓ   ⓫ Ⓐ Ⓑ Ⓒ Ⓓ   ⓴ Ⓐ Ⓑ Ⓒ Ⓓ

❸ Ⓐ Ⓑ Ⓒ Ⓓ   ⓬ Ⓐ Ⓑ Ⓒ Ⓓ   ㉑ Ⓐ Ⓑ Ⓒ Ⓓ

❹ Ⓐ Ⓑ Ⓒ Ⓓ   ⓭ Ⓐ Ⓑ Ⓒ Ⓓ   ㉒ Ⓐ Ⓑ Ⓒ Ⓓ

❺ Ⓐ Ⓑ Ⓒ Ⓓ   ⓮ Ⓐ Ⓑ Ⓒ Ⓓ   ㉓ Ⓐ Ⓑ Ⓒ Ⓓ

❻ Ⓐ Ⓑ Ⓒ Ⓓ   ⓯ Ⓐ Ⓑ Ⓒ Ⓓ   ㉔ Ⓐ Ⓑ Ⓒ Ⓓ

❼ Ⓐ Ⓑ Ⓒ Ⓓ   ⓰ Ⓐ Ⓑ Ⓒ Ⓓ   ㉕

❽ Ⓐ Ⓑ Ⓒ Ⓓ   ⓱ Ⓐ Ⓑ Ⓒ Ⓓ

❾ Ⓐ Ⓑ Ⓒ Ⓓ   ⓲ Ⓐ Ⓑ Ⓒ Ⓓ

0	0
1	1
2	2
3	3
4	4
5	5
6	6
7	7
8	8
9	9

1 Carrie knows the moon goes through a cycle of phases about once each month. Which is the correct order of phases Carrie would see in the night sky?

(A) first quarter → full moon → new moon

(B) third quarter → first quarter → new moon

(C) first quarter → full moon → third quarter

(D) full moon → new moon → first quarter

TEKS 4.8C

2 Peter wants to compare physical properties of matter, specifically mass. He places six balls of modeling clay on one side of a pan balance. He places a plastic cup on the other side and finds that it takes 41 plastic cubes to balance the modeling clay. He then removes the modeling clay, shapes it into a dinosaur, and puts it back on the pan balance.

How many cubes will he most likely need to put into the cup to balance the dinosaur?

(A) 35 cubes

(B) 38 cubes

(C) 41 cubes

(D) 47 cubes

TEKS 4.4A, 4.5A

3 Mr. Ramirez uses a Celsius thermometer to collect and analyze the temperature of a cup of cold water and a pan of boiling water. His class observes the two temperatures.

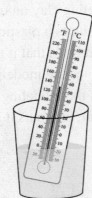

Which of the following sentences is a correct contrast of the two temperatures measured in Celsius?

Ⓐ The water in the glass is 30 degrees cooler than the water in the pan.

Ⓑ The water in the glass is 45 degrees cooler than the water in the pan.

Ⓒ The water in the glass is 82 degrees cooler than the water in the pan.

Ⓓ The water in the glass is 112 degrees cooler than the water in the pan.

TEKS 4.4A, 4.5A

4 Jayden is interested in how energy can be generated from the heat inside Earth's crust. Which science career would enable him to explore this interest?

Ⓐ biologist

Ⓑ hydrologist

Ⓒ electrical engineer

Ⓓ geothermal technician

TEKS 4.3D

5 Jin observes the weather one day. He observes and measures the changes in temperature, wind speed, air pressure, and humidity. Which of these best supports the prediction that it will rain soon?

(A) The air humidity is low.

(B) The temperature is 9 °C.

(C) The wind is light and from the south.

(D) The air pressure is 745 mm and falling.

TEKS 4.8A

6 Tyisha is contrasting her coin collection by physical properties of matter. Which physical property can she use to sort her collection of dimes and quarters?

(A) size

(B) color

(C) texture

(D) hardness

TEKS 4.5A

7 Hakim knows that it is important to conserve natural resources. One way to do this is to reuse materials. Which of the following is an example of a way that Hakim could make an informed choice in the reusing of materials?

Ⓐ turn off the lights when he leaves a room

Ⓑ turn jelly jars into containers for leftover food

Ⓒ turn off the water while he is brushing his teeth

Ⓓ turn off the air conditioner and open the windows

TEKS 4.1B

8 The bald cypress tree produces seeds that are protected within cones. This tree is found in Texas swamps, where heavy rains cause floods. The floodwaters spread the cones throughout the swamps. What role do the floodwaters play in the life cycle of the bald cypress?

Ⓐ pollination

Ⓑ fertilization

Ⓒ seed dispersal

Ⓓ removal of dead leaves

TEKS 4.10C

9 There are two main types of electric circuits: series circuits and parallel circuits. How are series circuits different from parallel circuits?

(A) A series circuit provides energy to one or two devices. A parallel circuit provides energy to many devices.

(B) In a series circuit, electrons flow in one direction. In a parallel circuit, electrons travel in both directions.

(C) A series circuit uses electrical energy from a battery. A parallel circuit uses power from an outlet or a generator.

(D) In a series circuit, there is only one possible path that electrons can follow. In a parallel circuit, there are two or more possible paths.

TEKS 4.6C

10 The table below shows how long it takes for various paper products to decompose in salt water. Interpret the data in the table.

Item	Decomposition time
Paper towel	2–4 weeks
Newspaper	6 weeks
Cardboard box	2 months
Waxed milk carton	3 months

Based on the patterns in the data, which explanation of decomposition time is most reasonable?

(A) A shoebox will decompose the fastest.

(B) A magazine will decompose the fastest.

(C) A cereal box will decompose the fastest.

(D) A paper napkin will decompose the fastest.

TEKS 4.2D

11 Hannah is planning a descriptive investigation on animal behavior. She decides to observe the behavior of birds in her backyard. Then she makes inferences about bird behavior from the observations she collects. What inference about animal behavior would she most likely make if she saw a female robin repeatedly carrying pieces of dried grass to the same limb of a tree?

(A) Robins eat dried grass.

(B) Robins make nests from dried grass.

(C) Robins use dried grass to attract mates.

(D) Robins are curious about objects such as dried grass.

TEKS 4.2A, 4.10A

12 Marcus is classifying resources by whether they are renewable or nonrenewable. Which of the following should he classify as two of Earth's nonrenewable resources?

(A) air and sunlight

(B) coal and natural gas

(C) water and natural gas

(D) sunlight and coal

TEKS 4.7C

13 Luis is studying force and motion. He designs an experiment using two balls, Ball 1 and Ball 2. The picture below shows the equipment that he is using.

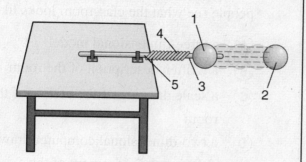

How does the energy of Ball 1 compare with the energy of Ball 2?

(A) Ball 1 and Ball 2 have no energy.

(B) Ball 1 has the same energy as Ball 2.

(C) Ball 1 has more kinetic energy than Ball 2.

(D) Ball 1 has more potential energy than Ball 2.

TEKS 4.6A

14 Frankie put one spoonful of brown sugar into a cup of hot tea. When will her mixture be a solution?

(A) when she adds the sugar

(B) when she stirs the tea

(C) when the tea begins to dissolve

(D) when the sugar is completely dissolved

TEKS 4.5C

15 Josie likes to visit the park in her neighborhood to watch hummingbirds. She often sees them find food from deep inside flowers.

Which feature of a hummingbird is most adapted to what the bird eats?

(A) the size of its wings

(B) the length of its legs

(C) the shape of its beak

(D) the color of its feathers

TEKS 4.10A

16 Dan is making a model of his classroom. He wants people to see what the furniture and other objects look like. Which of the following is the best model to use to help people see what the classroom looks like?

(A) a three-dimensional model

(B) a written description of the room

(C) a scale drawing of the outline of the room

(D) a two-dimensional computer drawing showing the placement of the furniture

TEKS 4.3C

17 Justin constructed the weather map below using current technology to organize, examine, and evaluate data.

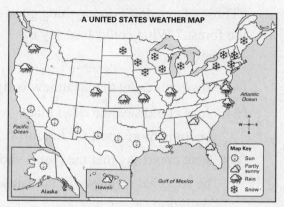

A UNITED STATES WEATHER MAP

Map Key
☼ Sun
⛅ Partly sunny
🌧 Rain
❄ Snow

He has his classmates use the map to predict the weather data for Texas. Based on the map key, what is the predicted weather for Texas?

Ⓐ sun

Ⓑ rain

Ⓒ snow

Ⓓ partly sunny

TEKS 4.2C, 4.8A

18 Identify Earth's renewable resources. Which of these generating stations uses a renewable source of energy?

Ⓐ coal plant

Ⓑ nuclear power plant

Ⓒ natural gas generator

Ⓓ hydroelectric generator

TEKS 4.7C

19 Chang plans a descriptive investigation by selecting and using appropriate equipment. He fills four cups with hot water. Then Chang measures the starting temperature of the water before covering the cups with four different materials. He measures the temperature again after 10 minutes. The table below shows Chang's results.

Material	Starting temperature (°C)	Final temperature (°C)
Wool fabric	80	74
Cotton fabric	80	66
Styrofoam	80	68
Plastic bubble wrap	80	71

What do Chang's results suggest?

(A) Wool fabric is the best insulator in his test.

(B) Wool fabric is the best conductor in his test.

(C) Cotton fabric is the best conductor in his test.

(D) Plastic bubble wrap is the best insulator in his test.

TEKS 4.2A, 4.6B

20 Matthew and José are on a forest field trip. They observe that the forest floor is covered with dead plants. Matthew says, "Those plants don't do anything good for the forest." What could José say to Matthew?

(A) José could say that Matthew is right.

(B) José could say that dead plants will become more food for the forest.

(C) José could say that the plants should be recycled so they will not cause pollution.

(D) José could say that cells in the plants will still use sunlight to produce more food.

TEKS 4.9B

21 In this food web, from where does the frog get energy?

- Ⓐ from the fish
- Ⓑ from the snail
- Ⓒ from the plant
- Ⓓ from the cricket

TEKS 4.9B

22 It bothers Meg that water collects in the soap dish and slowly dissolves the soap. She wants to use empirical evidence to critique the scientific explanation that soap dissolves in water. She designs a soap dish that water can drain from, and she makes a prototype. When she tests her prototype soap dish, what is the most important result she will watch for?

- Ⓐ how large it is
- Ⓑ how attractive it is
- Ⓒ how quickly water drains from it
- Ⓓ how much it looks like the old one

TEKS 4.3A

23 Maya is observing the growth of different bean seedlings. She places each seed on a wet paper towel and seals it in a plastic bag. She puts all the seeds in a warm place to germinate. After they germinate, she places one seed in the refrigerator, one in the middle of the room, and one on top of a hot radiator. Which scientific explanation is Maya using experimental testing to analyze?

Ⓐ Light affects plant growth.

Ⓑ Water affects plant growth.

Ⓒ Temperature affects plant growth.

Ⓓ Wet paper towels affect plant growth.

TEKS 4.3A

24 Sarai visits the local nature center. She sees a number of young animals. Which of the animals hatched from an egg?

Ⓐ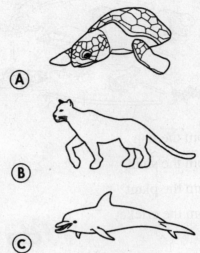

Ⓑ

Ⓒ

Ⓓ

TEKS 4.10C

25 Sam is studying force and motion. He designs an experiment that uses a piece of equipment that can send balls a short distance. The picture below shows the equipment that he used.

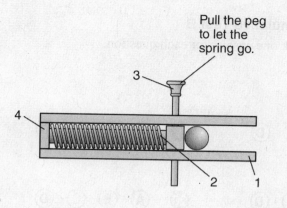

Pull the peg
to let the
spring go.

Which part of the equipment has the most potential energy?

TEKS 4.6D

Name _____ Date _____

Cumulative Test B

Mark one answer for each question.

❶ (A) (B) (C) (D)

❷ (A) (B) (C) (D)

❸ (A) (B) (C) (D)

❹ (A) (B) (C) (D)

❺ (A) (B) (C) (D)

❻ (A) (B) (C) (D)

❼ (A) (B) (C) (D)

❽ (A) (B) (C) (D)

❾ (A) (B) (C) (D)

❿ (A) (B) (C) (D)

⓫ (A) (B) (C) (D)

⓬ (A) (B) (C) (D)

⓭ (A) (B) (C) (D)

⓮ (A) (B) (C) (D)

⓯ (A) (B) (C) (D)

⓰ (A) (B) (C) (D)

⓱ (A) (B) (C) (D)

⓲ (A) (B) (C) (D)

⓳ (A) (B) (C) (D)

⓴ (A) (B) (C) (D)

㉑ (A) (B) (C) (D)

㉒ (A) (B) (C) (D)

㉓ (A) (B) (C) (D)

㉔ (A) (B) (C) (D)

㉕

(0)	(0)
(1)	(1)
(2)	(2)
(3)	(3)
(4)	(4)
(5)	(5)
(6)	(6)
(7)	(7)
(8)	(8)
(9)	(9)

Science Safety and Science Tools

Science Safety Quiz, pp. AG 1–5

1. D	9. D	17. A
2. D	10. C	18. C
3. C	11. D	19. C
4. C	12. D	20. B
5. A	13. D	21. B
6. C	14. B	22. C
7. C	15. A	23. B
8. D	16. A	24. C

Short Response

25. Students should accurately describe the location of the fire extinguisher and explain how to use it.

26. safety goggles, gloves, lab apron; Safety goggles are used to protect the scientist's eyes. Gloves and apron are used to protect his hands and clothes from chemicals.

27. Sample answer: If hair hangs loosely, it can contact chemicals or flames.

28. Sample answer: You should be careful when handling or touching living organisms. You should also be careful not to harm a living organism when studying it.

29. Sample answer: You should use soap and warm or hot water. You should soap up your hands thoroughly before rinsing them off and then drying them.

30. You should ask your teacher for help.

Science Tools Quiz, pp. AG 6–15

1. C	14. D	27. D
2. D	15. D	28. C
3. D	16. D	29. D
4. B	17. C	30. A
5. B	18. D	31. B
6. C	19. B	32. A

7. D	20. D	33. B
8. B	21. B	34. D
9. B	22. A	35. A
10. B	23. C	36. B
11. B	24. B	37. B
12. A	25. B	38. B
13. C	26. B	39. A

Short Response

40.

City	Mon.	Tues.	Wed.	Thurs.
Amarillo	12 kph	16 kph	2 kph	9 kph
Austin	15 kph	5 kph	22 kph	5 kph

41. Sample answer: You could use the net to collect fish and analyze how they are alike and how they are different.

42. 11:00 a.m.; 1:00 p.m.; 3:00 p.m.; 5:00 p.m.

43. 30 km/hour

44. Sample answer: Both balances can be used to find the mass of objects. A pan balance is used to compare the masses of two objects. A triple-beam balance is used to find the mass of one object.

45. Sample answer: It is important to track the procedure that you use and note any problems. It is important to record all data. It is important to keep notes and write conclusions and results.

Unit 1 Studying Science

Lesson 1 Quiz, p. AG 18
1. A   4. D
2. B   5. C
3. D

Lesson 2 Quiz, p. AG 19
1. C   4. B
2. A   5. D
3. B

Lesson 3 Quiz, p. AG 20
1. B   4. C
2. A   5. A
3. D

Lesson 4 Quiz, p. AG 21
1. B   4. D
2. A   5. A
3. C

Lesson 5 Quiz, p. AG 22
1. B   4. D
2. D   5. C
3. A

Lesson 6 Quiz, p. AG 23
1. A   4. D
2. C   5. D
3. B

Unit 1 Test, pp. AG 26–30
(3 points each)

1. A	7. D	13. D
2. D	8. A	14. A
3. C	9. D	15. C
4. D	10. C	16. B
5. B	11. D	17. C
6. C	12. A	18. B

Short Response
(8 points each)

19. Sample answer:
- Fran makes a model of a mountain by building a pile of sand. She makes a model of a flowing river by pouring water on the sand. Fran is not able to visit a real mountain but uses her model to investigate how rivers wash away soil.

To get full credit for this test item, students must include the following information:
- identification of the sand pile as a mountain model and the poured water as a river model
- an understanding that the models allow Fran to draw conclusions about what happens on a real mountain without having to visit one

20. Sample answers:
- The sentence is false. Anyone can think like a scientist. I would change the sentence to say that discoveries in science are made by both scientists and people who are not scientists.

To get full credit for this test item, students must include the following information:
- sentence is not true
- scientists as well as nonscientists can make new scientific discoveries

21. Sample answers:
- Meterstick: 127 cm
- Tape measure: 4'2"

To get full credit for this test item, students must identify a proper measuring tool and provide a reasonable measurement.

Extended Response
(11 points each)

22. Sample answers:
- Models are small replications of what happens in nature, such as a volcano made by combining baking soda and vinegar.

- Models can be flat, like making a footprint on paper, or 3-D, like making a diorama.
- Models are made to look like something in nature, such as showing what happens when two objects collide.
- Models show how things work in nature, such as a working model of a human heart.
- Models help us understand what happens in nature, like a model of how shadows are created.

To get full credit for this test item, students must identify size and accuracy as limitations of models.

23. 3 (3.35 cm)

Unit 2 The Engineering Process

Lesson 1 Quiz, p. AG 33
1. D   4. C
2. B   5. D
3. A

Lesson 2 Quiz, p. AG 34
1. C   4. C
2. B   5. A
3. D

Lesson 3 Quiz, p. AG 35
1. C   4. C
2. D   5. A
3. B

Lesson 4 Quiz, p. AG 36
1. C   4. A
2. A   5. C
3. D

Unit 2 Test, pp. AG 39–43
(3 points each)

1. A	7. C	13. A
2. C	8. D	14. C
3. A	9. A	15. B
4. B	10. C	16. B
5. A	11. C	17. D
6. B	12. B	18. C

Short Response
(8 points each)
19. Sample answer:
- The engineers should conduct multiple tests to evaluate their prototype and design. They should pay careful attention to the measurements and other data they collect.

To get full credit for this test item, students must recognize the importance of:
- collecting data by measuring
- analyzing the data
- performing repeated tests

20. Sample answer:
- The students should follow the steps of the design process to plan and build a prototype of their sled and keep good records of their work.

To get full credit for this test item, students must recognize the importance of following the steps of the design process:
- planning and building a prototype
- keeping good records and drawings

21. Sample answer:
- The engineers can use a computer or count the number of cars themselves. They can organize the data into tables of numbers.

To get full credit for this test item, students must recognize the importance of measurement:
- counting the number of cars
- selecting appropriate equipment or technology
- creating data tables

Extended Response
(11 points each)
22. Sample answers:
- The students must design a water bottle that will not be dropped easily. They should build a prototype, test it, and record their observations.

- The students need to design a water bottle that people can hold. They should create a new design and observe how it tests.
- The students must create a new type of water bottle. They should design a new one and describe what happens when people hold it while moving.

To get full credit for this test item, students must identify the problem and describe a design process that includes recording data.

23. 4

Unit 3 Matter

Lesson 1 Quiz, p. AG 46
1. B   4. B
2. D   5. A
3. C

Lesson 2 Quiz, p. AG 47
1. A   4. C
2. C   5. D
3. B

Lesson 3 Quiz, p. AG 48
1. D   4. A
2. A   5. C
3. B

Lesson 4 Quiz, p. AG 49
1. D   4. D
2. A   5. A
3. B

Lesson 5 Quiz, p. AG 50
1. B   4. A
2. D   5. D
3. C

Lesson 6 Quiz, p. AG 51
1. A   4. B
2. B   5. A
3. A

Unit 3 Test, pp. AG 54–58
(3 points each)
1. A   7. B   13. C
2. B   8. B   14. B
3. C   9. D   15. D
4. A   10. A   16. C
5. D   11. B   17. D
6. B   12. B   18. B

Short Response
(8 points each)
19. Sample answers:
- can see the parts of a mixture; sand in water
- Substances dissolve to form a solution; lemonade.
- A solution changes color as a solid dissolves in a liquid; powdered drink mix.
- can see the individual parts of a mixture; vegetable soup

To get full credit for this test item, students must explain the difference between a mixture and a solution and provide an example of a mixture or a solution.

20. Sample answers:
- Heat moves from the liquid into the ice, causing it to melt.
- Heat is transferred from the liquid and air to the ice.
- Ice turns to liquid water as it absorbs heat from the liquid.

To get full credit for this test item, students must explain that heat is transferred from the warmer liquid and surroundings to the ice, causing it to melt.

21. Sample answers:
- No; the same amount of matter exists in all states of the matter, although the volume changes.
- No; matter cannot be lost or destroyed, only changed.
- No; there would be the same amount of water in an ice cube as in the liquid water that forms when the ice cube melts.

To get full credit for this test item, students must show an understanding of the law of conservation of mass.

Extended Response
(11 points each)
22. Sample answers:
- The items can be placed into two groups based on hardness. The plate, penny, DVD, and button would go into the "hard group." The ball of yarn, tennis ball, and peach would go into the "soft group."
- The items can be grouped by volume, or the space they take up. The plate, ball of yarn, tennis ball, and peach would go in the "large volume group." The penny, DVD, and button would go in the "small volume group."
- The items can be sorted by mass. The penny, DVD, button, and ball of yarn would be in the "small mass group." The peach, tennis ball, and plate would be in the "large mass group."

To get full credit for this test item, students must categorize the items into two groups based on their similar physical properties and describe the properties used.

23. 92

Unit 4 Forms of Energy

Lesson 1 Quiz, p. AG 61
1. C
2. B
3. B
4. B
5. D

Lesson 2 Quiz, p. AG 62
1. D
2. C
3. B
4. A
5. B

Lesson 3 Quiz, p. AG 63
1. B
2. C
3. B
4. C
5. C

Lesson 4 Quiz, p. AG 64
1. D
2. A
3. B
4. A
5. C

Lesson 5 Quiz, p. AG 65
1. A
2. B
3. C
4. C
5. D

Unit 4 Test, pp. AG 68–72
(3 points each)
1. C
2. D
3. B
4. A
5. D
6. A
7. D
8. C
9. C
10. B
11. C
12. A
13. B
14. C
15. D
16. D
17. C
18. B

Short Response
(8 points each)
19. Sample answers:
- Stovetop: Heat is transferred from the heating element to a pot or pan by conduction.
- Furnace: transfers heat through convection as hot air moves in the rooms
- Heated floor: Heat is transferred by conduction from the floor to my feet when I walk on it.
- Fireplace: Heat is transferred from the fire to the air throughout the room by convection and directly by radiation.

To get full credit for this test item, students must identify a heat source and explain how heat is transferred from the source to a different place.

20. Sample answers:
- Wood: Wood is not a good conductor, so heat will not move through the walls easily.
- Wood: Metal is a better conductor than wood.
- Wood: It's a better insulator.
- Wood: It is thicker than metal and a better insulator.

To get full credit for this test item, students must identify wood as an insulator and metal as a better conductor of heat.

21. Sample answers:
    • Electrical energy is converted to sound energy.
    • Sound is created when electrical energy becomes sound energy.
    To get full credit for this test item, students must state that electrical energy is transformed into sound energy.

Extended Response
(11 points each)
22. Sample answers:
    • Heat moves from the burner to the pan to the liquid to the spoon. Gradually, the entire spoon gets hot.
    • Heat flows from the soup to the spoon, and then from the hot part of the spoon to the cooler part, so the whole spoon eventually gets hot.
    • The entire spoon gets hot when heat moves from the soup to the part of the spoon in the soup and then to the end of the spoon.
    To get full credit for this test item, students must recognize at least three areas of heat transfer.

23. 89

Unit 5 Electricity and Circuits

Lesson 1 Quiz, p. AG 75
1. A	4. D
2. B	5. C
3. A	

Lesson 2 Quiz, p. AG 76
1. B	4. D
2. D	5. D
3. B	

Lesson 3 Quiz, p. AG 77
1. B	4. A
2. D	5. B
3. C	

Unit 5 Test, pp. AG 80–84
(4 points each)
1. D	7. C	13. B
2. C	8. A	14. A
3. C	9. B	15. A
4. D	10. C	16. B
5. A	11. B	
6. C	12. B	

Short Response
(6 points each)
17. Sample answers:
    • The plastic paper clip acts as an insulator.
    • Metal is a conductor; plastic is an insulator.
    • Plastic is not a good conductor of electricity.
    • The plastic paper clip should be replaced with something made of metal.
    To get full credit for this test item, students must recognize that metal is a conductor and plastic is an insulator.

18. Sample answers:
    • turning off all lights when they are not being used
    • unplugging electronic devices when not in use
    To get full credit for this test item, students must identify a way they can conserve the natural resources used to produce electricity.

19. Sample answers:
    • to close the circuit and allow electrical energy to flow
    • to create a closed path through which current can flow
    • Without a conductor, the circuit will remain open.
    • You need a conductor to allow electricity to move in a loop.

To get full credit for this test item, students must recognize that the conductor allows electricity to flow in the circuit.

Extended Response
(9 points each)

20. Sample answers:
    * Wrap a copper wire around an iron nail several times and connect the free ends of the wire to opposite ends of a battery.
    * Use a nail, copper wire that has its covering removed, and a battery. Wrap the wire around the nail and connect the ends to the battery.

To get full credit for this test item, students must identify the need for a battery, nail (core), and copper wire and explain how the electromagnet would be constructed.

21. 3

Unit 6 Forces and Motion

Lesson 1 Quiz, p. AG 87
1. D   4. B
2. D   5. B
3. C

Lesson 2 Quiz, p. AG 88
1. B   4. C
2. D   5. D
3. A

Unit 6 Test, pp. AG 91–95
(3 points each)
1. C   7. C   13. D
2. D   8. B   14. C
3. A   9. A   15. A
4. A   10. D   16. B
5. C   11. D   17. B
6. D   12. B   18. C

Short Response
(8 points each)

19. Sample answers:
    * Speed is how fast something travels a given distance. Velocity includes both speed and direction of motion.
    * Speed does not take into account the direction in which an object moves. Velocity does.
    * Velocity is speed with direction.

To get full credit for this test item, students must understand that speed is how fast something travels, while velocity encompasses both speed and direction of motion.

20. Sample answers:
    * Gravity will be pulling down on the train, and friction will affect the train's speed.
    * If the train is on a track, friction will affect its speed, and gravity will keep the train on the track.
    * If it is an electronic train, magnetism moves it along the track, and gravity will keep it on the track.

To get full credit for this test item, students must identify two of three forces: gravity, friction, and/or magnetism.

21. Sample answers:
    * Gravity is a pulling force. Friction opposes motion between two surfaces that touch.
    * Gravity pulls things toward each other. Friction opposes motion when two things touch.
    * Gravity pulls objects toward each other. Friction acts in the direction opposite an object's motion.

To get full credit for this test item, students must recognize that gravity pulls objects toward each other, while friction opposes motion between surfaces that are touching.

Extended Response
(11 points each)

22. Sample answers:
    - One design would include different degrees of incline to test the effect of gravity on motion. The other design would include different surfaces to test the effect of friction.
    - Gravity and friction should be tested by changing the incline and surface of the skateboard ramps.
    - One ramp would be steep and smooth; the other ramp would have a lesser incline and be rough. The skateboarders would compare their test results to determine the effects of gravity and friction on motion.

    To get full credit for this test item, students should state that the effects of both gravity and friction should be investigated.

23. 19

Unit 7 Earth's Surface

Lesson 1 Quiz, p. AG 98
1. B   4. A
2. C   5. D
3. B

Lesson 2 Quiz, p. AG 99
1. C   4. D
2. A   5. C
3. B

Lesson 3 Quiz, p. AG 100
1. B   4. C
2. D   5. A
3. B

Lesson 4 Quiz, p. AG 101
1. C   4. D
2. A   5. B
3. B

Unit 7 Test, pp. AG 104–108
(3 points each)

1. B	7. C	13. D
2. C	8. B	14. C
3. A	9. D	15. B
4. D	10. C	16. A
5. D	11. B	17. A
6. A	12. D	18. A

Short Response
(8 points each)

19. Sample answers:
    - color, texture, ability to retain water, ability to support growth of plants
    - color, how the soil feels, how much moisture it can hold, and how well plants grow in it
    - how it looks and feels, how much water it keeps, and if plants can grow in it

    To get full credit for this test item, students must identify four unique properties of soil: color, texture, water retention, and ability to support plant growth.

20. Sample answers:
    - Many rocks contain tiny cracks.
    - When it rains, these cracks fill with water.
    - If the temperature drops, the water in the cracks turns to ice.
    - As ice is formed, it expands.
    - Over time, the repeated processes of freezing and thawing will cause these cracks to grow.
    - Eventually, the rocks will break apart.

    To get full credit for this test item, students must refer to the repeated expansion of water when it is frozen, slowly cracking the rock and pushing the pieces apart.

21. Sample answers:
    - Weathering is breaking down, and erosion is moving things away.
    - Weathering breaks things apart, and erosion moves them away.
    - Erosion carries away things that weathering breaks down.

To get full credit for this test item, students must understand that weathering is a breaking-down process and that erosion moves material from one place to another.

Extended Response

(11 points each)

22. Sample answers:
    - correct, because paper comes from trees
    - Trees are a renewable resource.
    - More trees can be planted to produce more paper.

To get full credit for this test item, students must identify that paper is often made from trees, indicate that trees are a renewable resource, and define a renewable resource.

23. 3; Water can cause slow changes to Earth's surface via weathering, erosion, and deposition.

Unit 8 The Water Cycle and Weather

Lesson 1 Quiz, p. AG 111

1. D   4. B
2. C   5. C
3. A

Lesson 2 Quiz, p. AG 112

1. D   4. C
2. B   5. A
3. A

Lesson 3 Quiz, p. AG 113

1. C   4. D
2. A   5. B
3. C

Lesson 4 Quiz, p. AG 114

1. B   4. D
2. C   5. C
3. A

Unit 8 Test, pp. AG 117–121

(3 points each)

1. B   7. A   13. C
2. C   8. D   14. A
3. D   9. A   15. B
4. B   10. B   16. D
5. B   11. C   17. B
6. C   12. D   18. D

Short Response

(8 points each)

19. Sample answers:
    - The sun is the main source of energy for the water cycle.
    - The sun provides energy for evaporation from Earth's surface.
    - The sun is important because it provides energy to the water cycle.

To get full credit for this test item, students must explain that the sun is the main source of energy for the water cycle process.

20. Sample answers:
    - use map symbols to identify weather systems
    - look for cold fronts, warm fronts, and areas of high pressure
    - see the way a front is moving and check for changes in temperature
    - decide what changes will occur when a front moves into an area

To get full credit for this test item, students must recognize that symbols on weather maps assist weather forecasters in making predictions and convey an understanding of how weather systems impact each other.

21. Sample answers:
    - Thermometer – measures air temperature
    - Barometer – measures air pressure
    - Rain gauge – measures amount of rain in a specific time period
    - Anemometer – measures wind speed
    - Hygrometer – measures water vapor content

To get full credit for this test item, students must identify two weather tools and describe the change in the weather each tool measures.

Extended Response
(11 points each)
22. Sample answers:
- Evaporation and transpiration release water vapor into the atmosphere.
- Water vapor cools to form clouds through the process of condensation.
- The water inside clouds becomes heavy and falls back to Earth's surface as precipitation.
- Surface runoff seeps into the ground to form groundwater.

To get full credit for this test item, students must correctly use each term when explaining the water cycle.

23. 31

Unit 9 Patterns in the Sky

Lesson 1 Quiz, p. AG 124
1. B   4. A
2. C   5. D
3. D

Lesson 2 Quiz, p. AG 125
1. C   4. B
2. C   5. D
3. C

Lesson 3 Quiz, p. AG 126
1. C   4. C
2. D   5. B
3. A

Lesson 4 Quiz, p. AG 127
1. A   4. B
2. D   5. C
3. D

Unit 9 Test, pp. AG 130–134
(3 points each)
1. C   7. C   13. A
2. D   8. B   14. C
3. A   9. A   15. A
4. D   10. D   16. B
5. C   11. C   17. C
6. B   12. D   18. B

Short Response
(8 points each)
19. Sample answers:
- causes tides to form
- causes the oceans to rise
- causes a tugging force on Earth's surface

To get full credit for this test item, students must show an understanding that the gravitational pull of the moon on Earth and Earth's waters is the major cause of tides.

20. Sample answers:
- between Earth and the sun
- revolving around Earth but between Earth and the sun
- between Earth and the sun so the moon looks dark or absent from the sky

To get full credit for this test item, students must recognize that during a new moon, Earth, the moon, and the sun are in line so that the face of the moon appears dark.

21. Sample answers (any four in sequence):
- new moon
- waxing crescent
- first quarter
- waxing gibbous
- full moon
- waning gibbous
- third quarter
- waning crescent

To get full credit for this test item, students must list four phases in the correct order, beginning at any point in the sequence. Students may skip any phase as long as four phases in sequence are identified.

Extended Response
(11 points each)

22. Sample answers (any two terms):
    - Shadows are longer before and after noon.
    - Shadows are shortest at noon and then grow longer until the sun sets.
    - Shadows are shortest during the middle of the day.

    To get full credit for this test item, students must correctly draw a shadow for each tree. The shadow at noon should be significantly shorter than the shadow at 9 a.m.

23. 9; Students should round up 8.89 to the nearest whole number.

Unit 10 Organisms and Their Environments

Lesson 1 Quiz, p. AG 137
1. B   4. A
2. A   5. C
3. C

Lesson 2 Quiz, p. AG 138
1. A   4. D
2. B   5. C
3. A

Lesson 3 Quiz, p. AG 139
1. D   4. B
2. A   5. D
3. C

Lesson 4 Quiz, p. AG 140
1. B   4. D
2. C   5. A
3. C

Unit 10 Test, pp. AG 143–147
(3 points each)

1. C	7. A	13. C
2. B	8. A	14. D
3. A	9. B	15. A
4. C	10. D	16. B
5. D	11. B	17. A
6. D	12. C	18. B

Short Response
(8 points each)

19. Sample answers:
    - main source of energy for the food chain
    - use energy from the sun to add energy to the food chain
    - provide energy for consumers

    To get full credit for this test item, students must show an understanding that producers are the main source of energy for most food chains.

20. Sample answer:
    - water, carbon dioxide, sunlight

    To get full credit for this test item, students must identify all three elements required for producers to make their own food.

21. Sample answers:
    - from the sun to producers to several consumers to decomposers
    - among many consumers that get energy from producers, who get energy from the sun
    - from an interaction of primary, secondary, and tertiary consumers
    - from the sun to one producer to several consumers that may eat different animals to get energy

    To get full credit for this test item, students must explain that in a food web, several consumers interact to gain energy that begins with energy from the sun providing producers with the ability to make food and grow.

Extended Response

(11 points each)

22. Sample answers:
  - Removal of the oak tree will reduce the mouse population and thus reduce the snake and hawk populations.
  - Removal of the mouse may reduce the snake and hawk populations but may increase the oak tree population.
  - Removal of the snake may reduce the oak tree and hawk populations but may increase the mouse population.
  - Removal of the hawk may increase the snake and oak tree populations and reduce the mouse population.

To get full credit for this test item, students must correctly explain how removing one organism from the food chain negatively or positively impacts the populations of the other organisms.

23. 4

Unit 11 Plants and Animals

Lesson 1 Quiz, p. AG 150

1. A   4. B
2. D   5. C
3. C

Lesson 2 Quiz, p. AG 151

1. C   4. A
2. C   5. D
3. B

Lesson 3 Quiz, p. AG 152

1. D   4. A
2. C   5. B
3. B

Lesson 4 Quiz, p. AG 153

1. D   4. B
2. D   5. A
3. C

Lesson 5 Quiz, p. AG 154

1. C   4. D
2. B   5. D
3. D

Lesson 6 Quiz, p. AG 155

1. A   4. C
2. D   5. B
3. C

Unit 11 Test, pp. AG 158–162

(3 points each)

1. A	7. C	13. B
2. C	8. D	14. A
3. D	9. D	15. B
4. B	10. B	16. C
5. A	11. A	17. D
6. B	12. D	18. B

Short Response

(8 points each)

19. Sample answer:
  - Desert plants have wide root systems that enable them to absorb a lot of water from infrequent rainfall. Desert animals avoid the heat of the day by being active at night.
  - Plants in rivers and streams have flexible stems that allow them to bend instead of break in the flowing water. Male penguins in the Antarctic instinctively huddle together, which helps the adults and their newly hatched offspring stay warm.

To get full credit for this item, students must provide one accurate example of a physical adaptation and a behavioral adaptation and explain how each helps the organism survive. The response should refer to one plant and one animal.

20. Sample answers:
  - need conditions that are right for germination, such as warm, moist soil
  - too cold and dry for germination
  - must have the right temperature and need rain before germination

To get full credit for this test item, students must recognize the need for proper soil conditions for germination, including moisture and soil temperature.

21. Sample answers:
    - The mother cat taught the kittens how to bathe themselves, so this likeness is learned, not inherited.
    - The kittens did not initially bathe themselves and displayed this behavior only after the mother demonstrated it. This is an example of a learned likeness.

    To get full credit for this test item, students must show an understanding that bathing is a learned behavior in cats.

Extended Response
(11 points each)

22. Sample answers (any two):
    - Desert hares have long ears and are brown. Arctic hares have white fur and short ears.
    - The long ears of desert hares allow heat to escape, while the short ears of arctic hares conserve heat.
    - Desert hares are brown to blend in with the desert environment, while arctic hares are white to blend in with the snow. This helps the hares survive by making it more difficult for predators to see them.

    To get full credit for this test item, students must correctly compare adaptations of the two hares, including fur color and size of ears, and note how the adaptations help the hares survive in their environments.

23. 3

Cumulative Test A, pp. AG 165–177

1. A	10. D	19. D
2. D	11. B	20. C
3. A	12. C	21. D
4. D	13. C	22. A
5. C	14. B	23. C
6. A	15. D	24. A
7. B	16. B	25. 2
8. C	17. D	
9. B	18. C	

Cumulative Test B, pp. AG 179–191

1. C	10. D	19. A
2. C	11. B	20. B
3. B	12. B	21. D
4. C	13. D	22. C
5. D	14. D	23. C
6. A	15. C	24. A
7. B	16. A	25. 2
8. C	17. A	
9. D	18. D	

Answer Key
© Houghton Mifflin Harcourt Publishing Company

AG 205

Grade 4 • Assessment Guide